T0285223

Freedom Teaching

Freedom Teaching

Overcoming Racism in Education to Create Classrooms Where All Students Succeed

Matthew Kincaid

JB JOSSEY-BASS™
A Wiley Brand

Published by John Wiley & Sons, Inc., Hoboken, New Jersey.
Published simultaneously in Canada.

For general information on our other products and services or for technical support, please contact our Customer Care Department within the United States at (800) 762-2974, outside the United States at (317) 572-3993 or fax (317) 572-4002.

Wiley also publishes its books in a variety of electronic formats. Some content that appears in print may not be available in electronic formats. For more information about Wiley products, visit our web site at www.wiley.com.

Library of Congress Cataloging-in-Publication Data is Available:

ISBN 9781119984832 (Paperback)
ISBN 9781119984849 (ePDF)
ISBN 9781119984856 (ePub)

COVER DESIGN: PAUL MCCARTHY
COVER ART: © GETTY IMAGES | OXYGEN

SKY10062329_121223

To my grandparents, Thelma, Thomas, Eugenia, and "Jack": You braved a world that I couldn't imagine and laid the foundation for everything that I could ever dream that I could become. Thank you.

To my students: Teaching you was the greatest honor of my life. This book and everything that I do is dedicated to you.

Contents

Contents

Introduction: The Journey

Our journeys as educators, activists, or anyone who desires to make change are often not linear. As a result of this there will be times in any activist's journey where it will feel like we aren't making progress at all. Much of what we learn in school about how significant change happens is focused on hero worship. We are socialized to believe that change occurs because a once-in-a-generation leader shows up and makes it happen. Because this is the way that our history books remember freedom movements, it is easy to trivialize our own ability to make change.

In the midst of my efforts to make change I have found myself falling into the trap of self-doubt. Who am I to believe that I am the one to move or shift systems that have been around for so much longer than I have? Systems that are so much bigger than I am? And systems that are so resistant to change? People read books written by experts, and my professional and educational experience would suggest that I am one of those. However, I actually think the story that needs to be told is a story of overcoming: overcoming doubt, overcoming real and perceived limitations, overcoming racism.

In my journey to overcome, I have found that the person who makes the most change isn't always the person who knows the most. Typically the people who make the most change are the ones who have the ability to cut through the noise. There is now, and has always been, a lot of noise around the topic of ending racism. One would think that everyone could get behind the idea that racism is bad and should be dug up from the roots in the systems that we all have to exist in. Instead, recently many states made it illegal to teach about racism in schools. Historically anti-racism advocates have faced ridicule, violence, false imprisonment, and in some cases, death. It goes without saying that the noise that surrounds anti-racism work is so loud that it is often deafening. The noise serves to paralyze us into cynicism, to keep us stuck in doubt, grief, or guilt. The noise aims to drown out our voices and make it harder for us to communicate with one another. Toni Morrison describes "the noise" this way: "the function, the very serious function of racism is distraction. It keeps you explaining, over and over again, your reason for being. Somebody says you have no language and you spend twenty years proving that you do. Somebody says your head isn't shaped properly so you have scientists working on the fact that it is. Somebody says you have no art, so you dredge that up. . . . None of that is necessary."[1]

The unjust structures and the people who support them are going to continue to do their work. Those of us who are inclined to create a just world for the students that we serve have to do our work too. We can only do this work as we are. We don't have the luxury to wait for someone else or to wait until we are a better version of ourselves. The heroes who are immortalized in our history books who led movements deserve all their praise, adoration, and credit. However, systems do not shift because of the actions of an individual. Systems shift because of committed individuals, imperfect individuals, the people the history books don't remember. Famed civil rights leader Ella Baker embodied this concept, saying, "You didn't see me on television, you didn't see news stories about me. The kind of role that I tried to play was to pick up the pieces or put together pieces of which I hoped organization might come. My theory is that strong people don't need strong leaders."[2]

There Is a Movement Inside You

The urgency of the moment dictates that we do not have the luxury of waiting for the once-in-a-generation leader. Instead, this book will encourage you to find the movement that exists inside of you. The battle for equity in education requires all of us to bring something important to this work. Your movement might not be mine. We need leaders both inside and outside of the classroom. We need a diverse set of skills, perspectives, and passions. If the education system is ever truly going to work in a way that serves all children, we need your movement—whatever it may be.

I often hold Overcoming Racism intensives where I talk about an activist named Dorothy Counts, who integrated schools in Charlotte, North Carolina, in 1957. On her first day of school, Dorothy Counts was met by a mob of upward of 300 angry white children and adults. Figures I.1 and I.2 show her being harassed by

Figure I.1 Dorothy Counts on her first day of school, Charlotte, North Carolina, 1957.

Photo by Douglas Martin, published September 5, 1957, in the *Charlotte News*. Public domain.

Figure I.2   Dorothy Counts on her first day of school, Charlotte, North Carolina, 1957.

Photo by Douglas Martin, published September 5, 1957, in the *Charlotte News*. Public domain.

her peers. Her first day of school was marked by her teachers ignoring her. Her classmates threw things at her, shouted racial epithets at her, and some boys even formed a circle around her at lunch and spat in her food. The district superintendent ignored her family's pleas to protect their daughter and the local police chief made it clear that he would do nothing to offer her protection. After four unbearable days at Harry Harding High, Dorothy's parents mercifully withdrew her from the school. By all accounts Dorothy, who is 81 now, is a hero. But when I ask participants in the Overcoming Racism intensives who she is, almost nobody recognizes her face.

The truth is I put this image of Dorothy Counts in the beginning of my presentations for completely selfish reasons. Dorothy Counts is a constant reminder to me of the sacrifices that people who look like me endured simply to get an equitable education. Dorothy was willing to put her entire community on her shoulders and face the rage and hatred of a bigoted crowd. Looking into the eyes of Dorothy Counts before I speak is a reminder that this work takes courage, and it has always taken courage. It is also a reminder that anti-racist change has never come without resistance, and that freedom has never truly been free. The breadth of Dorothy's bravery is only matched by the cowardice of the rageful crowd. What were they so afraid of, those three hundred people assembled to intimidate one high school girl?

I've been doing anti-racism work since I was 14. I've faced threats; I've been the target of white supremacists; I've faced police with tanks, dogs, and tear gas. My passion has always propelled me forward and the heroes who came before me have always strengthened my resolve. However, the years following the brief movement for Black lives following 2020 have been some of the most difficult. The swift transition from a widespread outcry against racism to the widespread passing of polices intended to reinforce racism is heartbreaking. In 2023, with half of the country passing laws targeting anti-racism training, for the first time in my activist journey I have considered what it would look like if I stepped away from this calling.

Black people have fought for centuries to have full enfranchisement in schools. My forebears shed literal blood, sweat, and tears simply to walk through the doors of institutions of learning that fought just as hard to keep them out. Both of my parents went to segregated schools for much of their childhood. I have always felt like it was my responsibility to do my part to make the world a little bit safer for my future children and all of the students I had the privilege to teach. As a historian, I have studied the centuries in which Black families were disallowed to attend schools, followed by the century of forced segregation, and I have lived my entire life in the decades of trying to make schools equitable for children who look like me. In the last year or so I have watched as, in what feels like a matter of months, white parents have organized to get books banned, to outlaw anti-racism training, and to undo centuries of hard-fought progress.

As I write this, half of the country has passed laws limiting the ability of schools to train their teachers in anti-racist practices. In the time in which I have committed my life to anti-racist change, I have felt pretty much every emotion imaginable. I have been afraid of driving past Confederate flags and plantations on my way to a rural workshop. I have been angry after being the target of misinformation and slander from white supremacists trying to discredit my work. I have felt joy and hope and love while watching the healing and liberatory nature of this work in schools. For the first time in my life, anti-racism work has broken my heart.

There is a part of me that won't stop crying for the fact that Dorothy had to face that crowd, and 66 years later people are using their positions of power to erase the fact that this happened from the history books. I say this all to emphasize that there is more work to be done. I have written this book for anyone and everyone who believes, like Dorothy did, that our students deserve an equitable education, no matter the cost. Dorothy Counts's story is not frequently told. It is a reminder to me that just because the history books don't remember you doesn't mean you didn't make a difference. In the end it's possible that not a single person remembers the name Matthew Kincaid or the work of Overcoming Racism. But just like Dorothy Counts, the change will endure. This book is for those courageous enough to pick up the torch that Dorothy, Ruby, the Little Rock Nine, and so many others lit and carry it, until our legs shake and our arms quiver, to its final destination. I know firsthand that the work ahead of us will be difficult, but I also know that it will be worth it. If teaching has taught me anything, it is that our students are the hope for the future and it's our job to build schools that are worthy of them.

Despite the crowd, Dorothy still marched forward. I cannot imagine the resolve that took. Who are we to turn around now?

Notes

1. Toni Morrison, "A Humanist View," Black Studies Center Public Dialogue. Pt. 2, Portland State University, Oregon Public Speakers Collection, May 30, 1975.

2. Ella Baker, "Jeannette Rankin News Conference," January 3, 1968, Washington, DC.

Chapter 1
Setting Intention

Race is everything and nothing at the same time. Somehow calling race what it is—a social construct—feels wildly inaccurate when faced with the reality of what humanity has created and maintained. I couldn't have been more than five years old when I was introduced to the illogical nature of race.

I grew up in a predominantly Black neighborhood, but went to majority white schools. Navigating these two worlds set up the foundation for this book. There is a common assumption that Black children first learn about race in the home, but my education on race came from school. It was actually my white teachers and peers who notified me that I was "Black" and it was also they who made me understand what being "Black" meant to many white Americans. At home everyone looked like me, most of the people in my neighborhood looked like me, and all of my extended family looked like me. Blackness was the norm and even at a young age I marveled at its beauty. Black love, Black family, Black ingenuity, Black excellence seemed to surround me at every turn. It wasn't until I started going to school that I learned the harsh lesson that many of my white peers were getting a different education on Blackness, or perhaps none at all; to this day I am not sure which is worse.

Perhaps my oldest memory of being in school is a white girl telling me that I could not play in the sandbox with the other children because I was "Black." She stood on the edge of the sandbox, arms outstretched pressed authoritatively against my chest. Surely the teachers, also white, noticed that the only Black child was playing alone on the playground, but they couldn't be troubled to intervene. Later that evening I told my mom about the encounter as we were heading into church. She paused, knelt down, grasped my shoulders affectionately, and began to give me "the talk."

At some point or another every Black parent in America has to have "the talk" with their children about what it means to be Black in America. There are rules. Some of the rules are to promote their child's success in an ecosystem that was not built with them in mind, but honestly most of the rules are about survival. I wonder what type of talk the young girl who guarded the sandbox was getting at home and if her parents knew that their hatefulness was spilling out of their young daughter at school. Looking back all of these years later after dedicating my life to teaching about race and racism, I am now firmly aware that the daughter's actions were the consequences of the education she received on race. This education had to be fundamentally different from mine.

In this way my first education on race came from my white teachers and peers. They taught me that being Black meant that I was "different." They taught me the stereotypes that I would spend the rest of my life sidestepping. And they taught me that Blackness came with an entirely different set of rules and expectations. As I learned to navigate whiteness at school, I also learned intrinsically just how silly race and racism are. Most notably, I learned that everyone loses in this system and that ending systemic racism is not just about liberating people of color; it is perhaps principally about the liberation of people who are white. I grew to love a lot of my white classmates and teachers and many of them loved me back, but love is not a sufficient antidote to ignorance—education is.

I am writing this book all these years later for the kid who had to learn to be comfortable in his skin at school. I am writing this book so that teachers and school leaders can envision and actualize schools that are physically and psychologically safe for all learners, especially learners of color. I am writing this book because for far too long we have settled with "the way things are," existing in a perpetual status quo in which large groups of students lose. I am not okay with this, and you probably aren't either if you picked up this book. Let's imagine a better present for our kids because their future depends on how we show up for them right now. It is my dream that we can no longer predict outcomes for students based on their race, gender, sexuality, class background, ability status—the list goes on. However, as Assata Shakur reminds us, "dreams and reality are opposites. Action synthesizes them."[1] Let's act in accordance with our purpose and let's lead the revolution of teaching for freedom.

Intention Matters

Take a moment to reflect on why you picked up this book. Ask yourself what you were hoping to get out of the experience of engaging with this text. In this book we will examine strategies and principles that promote the development of schools and classrooms that serve all children. Doing this requires us to approach this text with intentionality. If we are going to promote justice in education, we have to be as intentional as the systems, structures, and policies that have supported and maintained injustice. This is no easy task. If we as educators can get this right, then the sacrifice will be worth it.

At Overcoming Racism, before we engage with participants in learning intensives, we first go over some operating agreements. We used to call this practice "norm setting," but shifted to use of the word "agreements" because none of the learning in our intensives, or in this book, will stick if we cannot collectively agree to engage in a way that optimizes our learning together. Let's begin by examining the agreements, which will help you to get the most out of what this book has to offer.

Think of this as an active process. Reflect on whether you can agree to each of the following statements. Think about what it will require from you if the answer is yes, and reflect on what part of the agreement would need to change if the answer is no. Many of us signed up to be educators because we desire to positively impact the lives of young people while also playing our part in shaping our collective future. If you believe that our young people are too precious for us to continue to leave groups of children out, then continue to read. The journey ahead might be difficult, but belief is our first and most important hill to climb.

Agreement #1: Engage with Uncomfortable Truths

Year after year teachers go about the work of helping to raise the next generation. Of course our primary job is to educate them, but all teachers know that the job is so much more than that. Often, with inadequate resources and time, on any given day a teacher might be a parental figure, a counselor, a cheerleader, a nurse, a confidant. It takes a special person to sign up for and execute this job well. I like to believe that we don't see disparities because teachers, or students for that matter, don't care or aren't trying. Despite our best efforts, passion, and belief in our students, we still see students who have boundless potential fall short. This is an uncomfortable truth.

This book is going to engage a lot with uncomfortable truths. I will seek to tell the truth even when the truth might be hard to read. We will discuss topics that are uncomfortable and we will reflect on ourselves and our practice in ways that might unearth our complicity in systems that harm children. This can sometimes feel like it crosses the boundary between uncomfortable and unbearable. A part of the journey to find ourselves rooted in an education system that liberates students is first to liberate ourselves. This is not an easy process and it will require everyone reading this book to lean into and embrace the discomfort that comes with engaging with difficult truths. Truth comes before reconciliation, truth comes before justice, truth comes before freedom. The truth can hurt, but we can accomplish nothing until we learn to seek it with the same fervor with which we often run from it.

This comes up a lot in our work with teachers. Teachers are often already stressed and overburdened. Sometimes it feels easier to engage with the truths that make us comfortable. There are times in workshops when participants feel that, by being exposed to uncomfortable truths, we are dwelling on the negative, on what is, rather than discussing what could be. James Baldwin reminds us, "Not everything that is faced can be changed. But nothing can be changed until it is faced."[2] We will face ourselves in this book. We will face the condition of the education system in this book. We will face the tragic history that builds the foundation on which we are educating our students. Facing the truth, though difficult, gives us the ability to control our own destiny and that of our students.

If you are feeling cognitive dissonance, that is normal. Think about how uncomfortable learning can be for some of our students. Reading this book will not always feel good. Remember to reflect on why you picked the book up in the first place; hopefully one of those reasons was to challenge yourself. We are often socialized to place our individual comforts over a greater sense of collective justice. This book is the antithesis of that: we must place the pursuit of justice over our individual desire for comfort in order to pursue the change that we seek. In this way discomfort is not an unintended consequence of this work but rather a necessary hill to climb. Think about the times in your life when you have made your most personal growth; chances are those growth spurts coincided with challenges and moments of discomfort. In these moments of discomfort, reflect on the source of that discomfort and on how you plan to work through it. The truth is the truth and it doesn't change simply because we are uncomfortable with it. We are the ones who have to change and adapt until we can realize the new reality that we are fighting for.

Engaging with the uncomfortable truth that, despite our best efforts, the education system that we are existing in right now is not equipped to serve the needs of all children gives us the foundation to radically reimagine what is possible. We will reference reimagination often in this book, but perhaps more than anything our actual practice is what defines outcomes for students. If we think of our students as mirrors, reflecting back to us both the beauty of our practice as well as its imperfections, it becomes easier to see that changing outcomes for the students we serve starts with changing what we see in that reflection. This book will discuss in no uncertain terms the harsh realities of systemic injustice and oppression and the role that these systems play in educational inequality. Because we live in a society in which frank discussions on issues of oppression are socially discouraged, it will likely feel uncomfortable how directly we discuss them in this book.

Agreement #2: Replace a Scarcity Mindset with a Possibility Mindset

Scarcity is a fundamental reality of life. Educators know scarcity all too well, whether supplementing the school's budget with their own money to buy necessary supplies for their classrooms or trying to equitably share the limited number of minutes we have in our class with 30 different students with vastly different needs. A lot of our profession is about making masterpieces with what we have at our immediate disposal. We do an activity in our learning intensives in which we ask educators to envision what equity in education would look like. We preface this activity by asking participants to imagine without the constraints of a budget. We ask them to dream beyond what they think is possible or probable and to simply imagine what a school would look like, sound like, and feel like for students if equity were to truly be achieved.

This is a powerful activity because many of us are working toward an education system that we haven't even stopped to envision what it would actually look like if we were successful. It is almost like getting into your car and trying to drive to a destination without your GPS. You kind of know what it looks like but you have no idea how to get there. The most challenging part of this activity for our participants isn't the dreaming part; it is the fact that we ask educators to dream without limitations. Many of us are so conditioned to operate under real or perceived scarcity that we have lost some of our ability to dream beyond our own perceived limitations, or those of our students.

It is hard enough to change these systems that don't seem to want to budge without us making it harder on ourselves by buying a scarcity mindset. Especially when that mindset leads us to believe that if we are working to improve the experience for students whose needs have not been met for generations, that this somehow means we then need to choose a different student population to leave behind. If we engage in culturally responsive and sustaining practices in our classrooms that build self-esteem and improve performance for students of color, then somehow the opposite must now be happening for white students in the classroom. This is silly. This mindset has been one of the most consistent tools utilized to derail efforts for change. As long as we think of education as a zero-sum game in which some students win and others lose, we will always fall short of our calling. What are the material impacts of us deciding that we "can't make education equitable" because we don't know enough, we are not in the demographic of students, or because we are misaligned with leadership, or the like? At the end of the day our students need us to figure this out.

If there is one thing that teaching did for my life, it humbled me. It taught me how to empathize with how frustrating it can be to do something that is very hard over and over again. Failure is very hard for us as adults. For the most part, as we grow older we just stop doing the things that we aren't good at. Our students don't have that luxury, and for some of them, for various significant reasons, just showing up to school every day can be hard. Facing the anxiety of being a learner, especially in systems that weren't built with you in mind, can be extremely taxing. Existing in those environments daily, without having the agency to escape, could cause even the strongest of us to shut down. We ask students to do hard things on a daily basis. The goals we are hoping to accomplish in this book will require a lot of hard work. The genesis of this work starts in our mind. It starts with imagining what is possible rather than dwelling on all of the reasons our journey ahead will be difficult.

Agreement #3: Embrace Your Radical Imagination

This book is going to spend a lot of time discussing how we overcome the realities that systems of oppression place in our laps and the laps of our students. There are a lot of things that make facing systems of oppression extremely difficult. There are also a lot of things that work in our favor in this essential battle for the soul of our nation and its institutions. One of those things is that systems of oppression are predictable: patriarchy, white supremacy, ableism, classism, the list goes on. All of these systems maintain themselves by engendering hopelessness in individuals who would otherwise use their power to advocate for justice and change.

Systems of oppression are literally designed to steal from us our ability to hope beyond our current lived reality. Have you ever stopped to think about how we define what is and isn't "radical"? It is *radical* to envision an education system in which all students have access to healthy food options for lunch, access to safe places to play, and so on. However, it is not *radical* to exist in a school system where students can find themselves in debt because they can't afford school lunch. It is *radical* to imagine an education system in which students of color see themselves represented equitably in the curriculum and content of lessons. It is not *radical* for some students of color to go through their entire K–12 education without ever having read a book or engaged with a series of lessons that center their cultural experiences. It is *radical* to explore ways in which we can close gaps in achievement that are directly tied to access to resources and opportunities. It is not *radical* to exist in a school system in which your zip code is one of the most predictable indicators of your eventual SAT/ACT score. It is, however, *radical* to believe that students from all racial backgrounds, all socioeconomic classes, genders, sexualities, abilities, and so on should have an education system that works for them. These are children—it is time that we stop allowing them to carry the burden of generations of failed practices and policies so that they can dream of and actualize a better future for us all.

One of the things that white supremacy is designed to steal from us is our ability to believe in something better. Every single victory that has been won in this country for oppressed people has happened because people had the audacity to imagine and hope for it. The right to be free, the right to own land, the right to vote, the right to sit at the front of the bus, and yes, even the right to educate oneself at one time or another—these possibilities were all . . . *radical*. This book will discuss ideas that sound ambitious, perhaps even impossible if we fail to adjust our expectations. Paulo Freire reminds us that "it is imperative that we maintain hope even when the harshness of reality may suggest the opposite."[3] We will come back to this mantra time and time again as we journey through this book.

Agreement #4: Center Students

Students are the reason why we educate. Students are the reason why we have a profession and they are the reason why we stick it out even when we feel undervalued. Suggesting that students should be centered in their education is in no way revolutionary, unless we consider the fact that many of our systems, structures, and policies in schools center on adults. Schools that embraced the "no shortcuts, no excuses model" theorized that longer school days, restrictive dress codes, and punitive discipline systems would be the pathway for success for students. All of these policies, at their core, focus on the adult more than the student. Is it true that a child can't learn if their hair is styled a certain way? Or if their shoes aren't solid black? Is it truly in the best interest of the child to hold a student out of instructional time because they didn't bring their belt to school that day? Of course it isn't.

The aforementioned rules aren't about students; they are about creating a restrictive environment in which the belief is that it is easier for teachers to teach, especially teachers who are inexperienced. I completely understand why suspensions are an effective intervention for adults. An adult needs a break from a certain student because they are struggling to build a relationship with the student and the student is misbehaving. Those two or three days in which the student is away can feel liberating to the adult, who otherwise seems to have control over their class. However, I have yet to find a single study or educator in all my travels who could articulate how suspensions serve students. If the root of misbehavior is unmet needs, then what need does a suspension serve?

One of the main reasons students misbehave is because they have anxiety in the academic setting. If a student is behind academically, that often serves to increase that academic anxiety. If a student is acting out because they are feeling anxiety as a result of the academic content, removing them from hours of instruction only serves to increase said anxiety. If a student is acting out because they are dealing with problems at home, taking them out of the school environment and sequestering them in their home doesn't address that problem either. This is usually the part when defenders of exclusionary punishment systems remind me that suspensions are deterrents for bad behavior. However, the students who have the impulse control to weigh the costs and benefits of their actions prior to engaging in the undesired behavior are rarely in the population of students who are suspended. Exclusionary punishment systems are just one of many examples of systems that exist in schools that are supposed to support student behavior but instead mainly center adults. Saying that our thinking, our systems, and our structures should center students is by no means revolutionary, but acting in accordance with this edict is. When student needs are taken care of, everything else in a school follows. The strategies suggested in this book are unapologetically student-first.

Notes

1. Assata Shakur, *Assata: An Autobiography* (Chicago: Lawrence Hill Books, 2001), 275.
2. James Baldwin, "As Much Truth As One Can Bear," *New York Times*, January 14, 1962, https://www.nytimes.com/1962/01/14/archives/as-much-truth-as-one-can-bear-to-speak-out-about-the-world-as-it-is.html.
3. Paulo Freire, quoted in bell hooks, *Teaching Community: A Pedagogy of Hope* (New York: Routledge, 2003), 13.

Chapter 2
Freedom Teaching's Foundation

We all have different views about the ultimate purpose of education. Perhaps the goal is to improve students' upward mobility. For some it is about creating active and engaged citizens. For others it is about the noble pursuit of knowledge. These differing viewpoints make it difficult to define and work toward a common goal across a vast and diverse education system that in theory should work for all kids. Further complicating this dynamic is the reality that different students come from different backgrounds, have different wants, needs, and experiences, and their goals have to fit into the broader goals of the education system. To further complicate this, the opinions of parents, politicians, and external stakeholders also shape the overall goals and purpose of education. In this complex matrix of hopes and dreams, students are often lost in the process. As a result, injustice in our education system and predictable and preventable education disparities persist in perpetuity.

Education at its core should expand students' freedom. Choice and opportunity are an extension of freedom. I have come to learn in my work with students and schools around the country that our students who struggle aren't lacking in knowledge; they are

11

lacking in opportunities and choice. I have learned in some of the "best" educational environments that money can buy, "elite" institutions of learning, and what separated my classmates from the students I taught wasn't intellect or ability; it was the breadth of choices that stood in front of them. So many reforms in schools focus on "fixing" children as if the children themselves are broken. Freedom teaching is about examining a system that both historically and presently provides a vastly different array of choices and opportunities for students across lines of difference. Once that system is fully examined, we can go about fixing it and ensuring that it works for all students.

As an educator I had several hopes and desires for the students that I served. I wanted my students to attain a higher education; I wanted them to find meaningful and fulfilling work; I wanted them to be financially literate and sustained. I wanted them to make healthy choices about their diet, the media they consumed, and the social circle they inhabited. So I viewed my job as an educator as a practice in expanding my students' freedom. If one of my students didn't seek a higher education, I wanted that to be because that is the choice that they made, not because they didn't have the grades, the test scores, or the necessary skills. My students had every right not to take the AP level of my course in high school, but if that was the case I wanted that to be because they chose not to take the course, not because they struggled with document analysis or writing skills. This is why this book equates choice and opportunity with freedom, and the work we do on behalf of our students should be about expanding their ability to make life-altering choices.

Several very real lived realities impact why some students have a wider array of choices in their lives outside of school. The persistent and generational impacts of racism, sexism, classism, heterosexism, and all intersecting systems of oppression have a great impact on the choices students have before them. One student's refrigerator at home is filled with healthy food options, while another student's refrigerator might be completely bare. One student's home might have shelves full of books, while another student's home may have no books at all. One student might have access to high-speed Wi-Fi at home, while another student may need to find public Wi-Fi. One student may come from a lineage in which many generations attended college, while another student's family has yet to add attending college to their family's heritage.

So with different lived realities come different opportunities and choices. As the people entrusted with the education of these young people, it is our job to the best of our ability to correct for the opportunity gaps that exist outside of school. This book is about creating educational environments that expand students' freedom by expanding their inventory of choices and opportunities.

What Is Freedom Teaching?

If you ask, "What is the goal of teaching?" you get a different answer depending upon whom you ask. Some believe that the goal of teaching is to build students' knowledge of the world and how it operates. Others suggest that the goal of teaching is to instill positive character values. Perhaps teaching is simply a vehicle to create more productive and engaged members of society. Some might suggest that there are those who believe that the purpose of teaching is to increase students' earning potential.

All of the aforementioned goals have their merit. Although freedom teaching can be a vehicle to accomplish some of those goals, they are not the central driver of freedom teaching. The word "freedom" also means different things to different people. For some cultures, "freedom" is an individualistic ideal. As a result of this, many people are socialized to believe that other people's freedoms are a threat to their own. This scarcity-based mindset is the foundation of systemic oppression: the idea that freedom is something to hoard rather than something to share. The *Oxford English Dictionary* defines freedom as the "right to act, speak, or think as one wants without hindrance or restraint."[1] This definition defines freedom as a "right" but it doesn't get us closer to understanding who has the power to give that right or take that right away. Students certainly aren't allowed to act, think, or speak however they want without hindrance or restraint in schools, so does this mean that students are not or cannot be free? This causes me to pause to question whether freedom is a right, a practice, a state of being, or something different entirely. What does it genuinely mean to be free? If it is an ideal worth fighting for, then what does it mean for students to genuinely be free inside and outside of schools?

In order to find a version of freedom worth fighting for, I consulted several leaders who have worked to enhance their freedom and the freedom of others and I began to notice a trend.

Nelson Mandela on freedom:

- "I cherish my own freedom dearly but I care even more for your freedom."[2]
- "For to be free is not merely to cast off one's chains, but to live in a way that respects and enhances the freedom of others."

Rosa Parks on freedom:

- "I would like to be remembered as a person who wanted to be free . . . so other people would be also free."
- "I believe we are here on planet Earth to live, grow up, and do what we can to make this world a better place for all people to enjoy freedom.

Assata Shakur on freedom:

- "It is our duty to fight for our freedom. It is our duty to win. We must love and support one another, we have nothing to lose but our chains."[3]

Toni Morrison on freedom:

- "The function of freedom is to free someone else."[4]

Bayard Rustin on freedom:

- "If we desire a society in which men are brothers, then we must act towards one another with brotherhood. If we can build such a society, then we would have achieved the ultimate goal of human freedom."[5]

What these definitions of freedom have in common is that they present a version of freedom that is dependent upon expanding the freedom of others. Freedom teaching means creating schools that center students' collective liberation. Freedom teaching means creating schools where students can learn, grow, and achieve while also imagining their education as a gateway to a better life for themselves and those around them. In our work with schools I frequently hear teachers talk about preparing their students for the "real world." I have witnessed the justification of several unjust systems because "students have to get ready for the real world." What this basically amounts to is exposing young people to traumatic experiences in the name of preparing them to navigate the brokenness in our society. Freedom teaching instead views the world as malleable and teaches students that they have a say in the "real world" that they will both shape and inherit. Freedom teaching is about creating schools that reflect the society that we want our students to live in rather than reflecting the society that currently exists. For this reason, this book will speak directly about replacing oppressive systems with liberatory ones and expanding the definition of what we consider to be "success" to include a culturally sustaining education for all children.

There are no perfect strategies or absolutes when it comes to improving schools. Every context is different, every school is different, and every student is different. Our goal isn't to offer foolproof solutions; the goal is to offer a change in the way that we think about and approach problems.

Changing systems is rarely linear, despite our expectation that it is. There is a reason why after every school year successful teachers review their year and plan for the year ahead. If teaching were linear, one could just roll out the same lesson plans from the year before along with the same teacher moves and strategies. The reality is that we are as good as our preparation.

There is perhaps no more noble a calling than to dare to dream beyond the artificial boundaries set before us that leave us bound to systems that do not serve us—any of us. Indigenous, Black, white, male, female, cis, trans, neurotypical, neurodivergent—oppressive systems trap us all. The mission of creating an education system that serves all students is too critical to lose. Continuing the status quo means replicating a system that we know is designed to fail certain populations of students over and over again. Things that happen in cycles or patterns are usually not unintended. At the very least it is our duty to interrupt problematic cycles when we recognize them. It is time to stop pretending that educational inequity is a passive problem. Once we recognize that anything short of a revolution in education means to be complicit with oppression, we can claim our power to create a system that serves all students.

Theory of Change

When we start with the foundational belief that our students are not broken vessels in need of fixing, we can turn our focus to fixing the systems that students exist in. If we resign ourselves to believing that we don't have the agency to change outcomes for our students, we lose the battle. Alternatively, when we embrace our power to create the environments in which our students can thrive, we begin to realize just how much power we have to improve outcomes for the students we serve. By modeling for our students our ability to envision and actualize actively anti-racist environments, we empower them to do the same.

Change the Environment, Change the Outcomes

We are in charge of the environment that we cultivate for our students. We must be meticulous about creating an environment that is conducive to learning and care. When students step into our classrooms, we have to remember that we are not just teaching them but we are an extension of their parents; we are also helping to raise them. During the school year students spend just as much time with their teachers—if not more—as they do with their parents or guardians. Thus, in the time that we have them it is critical that we put them in an environment where they can thrive academically, socially, and emotionally. To illustrate this, in Overcoming

Racism workshops Ahmed Ahmed, our director of impact, frequently uses the metaphor of a garden. He asks, "How do you know whether or not someone is a good gardener?" Simply put, by looking at their garden. Are there some things that all good gardeners do to ensure a lush and healthy garden? Probably, but I imagine if you were to ask successful gardeners for a step-by-step guide on how to grow and maintain a garden you might get different answers or different approaches. The gardener is the variable, but the plants are the constant. Different plants need different things and no matter what tips, secrets, or techniques a gardener might employ, they must adhere to the specific needs of the plants that they are growing.

Gardening, like teaching, is difficult for beginners because different plants have different needs. Knowing and understanding the needs of the plant is critical to the plant's care. Some plants need constant sunlight, other plants prefer the shade. Some plants need water daily; others will wilt and discolor if you water them too much. Some plants have such need for sunlight that they will stretch their stems out of the shade to reach the sun. Other plants do just fine in the shade and don't require the warm touch of the sun. Anyone who has attempted to develop a green thumb knows that the environment is essential to a plant's care.

In the same way, students are nurtured in environments that acknowledge and affirm their culture as well as environments that take an intentional stance against systems of oppression. We often become so hyper-focused on teacher actions that we forget to look to the best barometer of our success in the classroom, the outcomes of our students. For years in education the focus has been on equality: just give all students the same thing. Intuitively this feels like the fairest path. So the goal in closing gaps in achievement has been about achieving equality rather than equity. However, equality inherently means that some students' needs will be met and the needs of others will not. Some students will be pushed to become the best version of themselves and others will not. Some people seek to make equity-based education a nefarious thing. It is not revolutionary to recognize that we serve culturally, ethnically, and socially diverse students, and consequently we need a culturally, ethnically, and socially diverse education system. If you wouldn't water an orchid like you water a fern, then perhaps the one-size-fits-all solutions in classrooms and schools exclude under the appearance of inclusion.

As educators, we have a responsibility to take ownership over what we can control while recognizing the things that we cannot. We are in control of the classroom environment. My first principal, Adam Meinig, used to implore teachers to be the thermostat and not the thermometer—the instrument that sets the temperature, not the one that simply measures it. Students are far more likely to adapt to the culture of the classroom than the culture of the classroom is to adapt to the students that are in it. Teachers and schools that struggle often find themselves blaming the students they serve for those struggles.

It is critical to remember that our students are a reflection of our practice. In my second year of teaching there was a particular class that I struggled with mightily. I was finally starting to feel like I was beginning to hone my craft; days were breezing by and I was racking up wins with most of my students. Yet without fail, every day my third-period class gave me the blues. The lessons we whipped through in other classes dragged on in this one. Some days it seemed like I fussed more than I taught. Instead of being in partnership with these students, I prepared for battle with them daily. I became frustrated and it wasn't long before I came up with excuses for why I was struggling with this class specifically. The problem couldn't be with me; I was doing the same thing in my other classes and I wasn't having these types of problems, so it had to be the students in this class. I thought about asking at the next grade-level meeting for the students to be split up, or for me to receive inclusion support like the students received in their math and English language arts classes. I wasn't sure what needed to change, but surely it wasn't me.

One day during my planning period I decided to observe this class with another teacher—a master teacher, our band instructor, Mr. Hart. I observed these students in a structured, nurturing, and culturally responsive environment. The students with whom I struggled were engaged in rigorous tasks. The undesirable behaviors that seemed unavoidable in my classroom were nonexistent in his. Most notably, the classroom wasn't just quiet or compliant; it was a thriving ecosystem of the students' personalities harmonizing like the music that flowed from their instruments. Mr. Hart's class did not change the dominant personalities that existed in this group; he just harnessed their energy in positive ways. The students who struggled to sit still or stay in their seats in my classroom played instruments that channeled that movement. Students who were talkative in my classroom led sections of the band. Students who seemed disinterested or apathetic in my classroom were paired with students who needed support, which drove their engagement.

The reality is that I went to that classroom to see how a veteran teacher "managed" the misbehaviors that were so prominent in my classroom. Yet I discovered that in Mr. Hart's class, those misbehaviors were not there. At that moment I realized that the students weren't the problem—I was. When placed in an environment that was curated with their particular personalities in mind, these same students who were consistently unsuccessful in my classroom thrived in another teacher's classroom. This was a humbling experience, but it taught me that the next step in my evolution as an educator was to shift the lens of my camera away from my actions and toward student outcomes.

Adjust the Camera Angle

A majority of teacher education and coaching points its "camera" at the actions of adults in the classroom. There are entire teaching guidebooks that focus on the "10 skills" or the "10 steps" that adults can take in their classroom to improve classroom culture. These widely applicable tips can be helpful for teachers who are starting out and are trying to master the science of teaching. The art, however, often requires more nuanced, personalized, and intentional approaches. We can get so fixated on the moves or actions we are taking in our classrooms that we forget that the ultimate test of whether our actions have meaning is in the outcomes we see with our students. This is the same principle I described above. We know how good a gardener is by looking at their garden. Equity is about the destination; it is inherently an outcomes-oriented process. We will know if the actions we are taking in the classroom are effective if students are learning, growing, and meeting their goals.

Anyone who has ever spent time coaching teachers has been in a classroom where the teacher was doing "all of the right things" but students still weren't learning at an appropriate pace. I've seen teachers who knew how to plan well, who practiced effective circulation, and who implemented systems and rules while holding students accountable to high expectations, yet they still run ineffective classrooms. It is difficult in a coaching session to tell a teacher that, from a technical standpoint, they aren't really doing anything wrong. Yet if we dig some more, we realize that despite the teacher doing a lot of the "right" things, there were specific students' needs that were not being met. Perhaps this teacher hadn't been intentional about building and maintaining relationships with students or with their parents or their guardians. Maybe this teacher wasn't effectively differentiating for students who were more advanced or were being left behind by the content. Possibly the teacher hadn't put time in building classroom investment systems or hadn't invested students into their specific content.

Focusing solely on teacher actions is another pathway toward deficit thinking about students. Once we decide that we are doing "everything right," then the next conclusion is usually that the students are doing something critically wrong. So the assumption in freedom teaching is that if we are actually doing everything "right," then that would be reflected in student outcomes. So we should backward-plan for the outcomes that we want to see in our schools and classrooms—outcomes like student well-being, student academic achievement, student critical consciousness, cultural consciousness, and so on. Determine which student behaviors drive those outcomes and adjust practices accordingly. Student outcomes should feed teacher inputs.

Dr. Gloria Ladson-Billings defines "culturally responsive pedagogy" as pedagogy that drives academic achievement, cultural competence, and critical consciousness.[6] Overcoming Racism has worked with countless partners who have struggled to get traction with practices that they believed to be culturally responsive. Some schools go as far as suggesting that they have "tried" culturally responsive pedagogy and it didn't work so they found themselves returning to traditional dominant pedagogical practices. Freedom teaching's response to this is that if you didn't see improvement in students' academic achievement, cultural competence, and critical consciousness, then that is evidence that the inputs or teacher behaviors were in fact not culturally responsive to begin with.

Use the Right Tools

Once we have determined the student outcomes that we want and the student behaviors that drive those outcomes, we can determine which teacher tools we should use to achieve those outcomes. Imagine a contractor throwing tools into a toolbox to travel to a job before knowing what the job was. Or a mechanic haphazardly picking out parts to fix a car without knowing what needed to be fixed. Or even worse, imagine a carpenter showing up to build a deck and bringing only a hammer, or only a saw. Teachers with the deepest toolboxes have the most success with the greatest number of students. Those are your veteran teachers, the ones who keep learning and adapting with each new class that comes into their classroom, the ones who cause you to sit back and marvel at how skillful they are in the classroom. It takes time, success, and failure to develop a deep and vast teacher toolkit. For teachers who are new or feel like their teaching has stagnated, deepening their toolkit is very important to the well-being of their classroom. In the meantime, however, having the wherewithal to choose the right tool for the right situation is perhaps even more important than having all of the tools in your toolbox.

I have taught in and observed schools where the response to almost every undesirable student behavior is to bring down the hammer. Students aren't quiet enough in the hallway, so let's enforce policies that make the hallway silent. Students aren't completing enough assignments, so let's relegate them to forced study halls and detentions. Students aren't meeting dress code expectations, so let's hold them out of class until they do or pass even more restrictive dress code policies. How often do we find ourselves escalating problems with students because we refuse to assess the situation and find the appropriate tool to get to the outcome that we ultimately want? If a kid is a nail then by all means pull out the hammer from time to time. But most students don't respond well to aggressive, repressive, or overbearing authoritative leadership.

The reality is that a majority of students will comply with whatever system we implement in schools. How do I know this? Well, if students stop complying en masse, then you are no longer running a school. We cannot simply accept compliance for alignment. Just because students are willing to fit under a certain system does not mean that it is the optimal system to maximize their growth. Freedom teaching means identifying the gap we are trying to fill, the problems we are trying to solve, and the realities we are trying to actualize. Once we identify our destination, then we start to assemble the tools we need to get there. Every time we make a decision that has an impact on students, we should ask ourselves over and over again what problem we are trying to solve. At the very least this should limit the number of times we find ourselves employing low-leverage interventions simply because they are the interventions that we are used to or comfortable with.

Legendary educator Rita Pierson gave one of the first viral education TED talks. During this talk, called "Every Child Deserves a Champion," she illustrates a scene in which a student fails an assessment by getting all but two answers incorrect. She puts a "plus two and a smiley face" on his paper. When he sees her marks on the assessment the student asks, "Ms. Pierson, is this an F?" When she responds "yes," the audience breaks out in laughter. Rita Pierson then delivers an iconic line: "You see, minus 18 sucks all of the life out of you; plus 2 says, 'I ain't all bad.'"[7] The emphasis here is on building up this student to review the content and to master it on his retake or his next assessment. Rather than seeing the assessment as a destination, Rita Pierson saw it as a checkpoint and she relayed that sentiment to the student masterfully.

A few years ago I was leading a workshop in Miami and decided to show this clip in the workshop. After the clip was over, a first-year teacher raised her hand and I called on her. She remarked flatly, "That doesn't work." Caught a little off guard, I asked, "What do you mean?" She responded that she had seen this clip before, tried the intervention with a student, and the student responded by ripping up his paper. After doing my best to reassure the teacher that we've all been there before and things get better, I took the time to remind the participants in the workshop of the real power behind the clip and the strategy. It wasn't simply that Rita Pierson had this tool in her toolkit; it is that she identified the right student to use it with and the right moment to employ it. If this was a strategy that Rita Pierson used with all of her students, then the student wouldn't have registered surprise when she marked his paper the way that she did. As famous as this exchange is, there were likely several students in the classroom for which this would have just been bad teaching.

But Rita Pierson's entire talk was about the value of relationships. She had a good enough relationship with this student to know that a big red F on the top of his paper would have likely caused him to shut down. So this is a great example of Rita Pierson asking herself what the gap was and what tool she needed to fill that gap. The gap was the student's mastery of the subject material. At the end of the day the student's grade on that assessment is informative but ultimately irrelevant to what Rita must do next to get the student to master the content. So she digs into her tool belt and uses a strategy that focuses on the student outcome she is trying to actualize.

There are several lessons in the retelling of this one exchange: lessons about empathy, lessons about finding creative solutions, lessons about building student self-esteem. All of those are made possible because Rita Pierson is a freedom teacher and freedom teachers use the right tools for the job in front of them.

Freedom Teaching's Five Tenets and How to Use Them

- Maintain hope that is radical.
- It isn't rigorous if it isn't relevant.
- Free minds, free kids.
- Trouble doesn't teach.
- Cultivate a classroom that values cultural wealth.

Each of the chapters that follow will elaborate on a different tenet of freedom teaching. The goal of freedom teaching is to create educational environments that liberate students and in turn enhance their ability to make choices that give them control over critical elements of their lives. Freedom teaching tenets and techniques are not intended to be used as a magic wand or a cure-all for all of the issues in our education system. The assumption is and will always be that you as the reader of this text know more about the individual context of your school, classroom, city, or state than I do. So when teaching or employing freedom teaching tenets, please use the following principles as your guide.

FREEDOM TEACHING REQUIRES INVESTMENT IN BOTH THEORY AND PRACTICE. Freedom teaching is about finding the intersection between theory and practice. Using this text to provide a theoretical framework without engaging in the practice of employing the techniques likely won't yield the results you want. Engaging solely in the practices without internalizing the theory also will yield incomplete results. One of the reasons why anti-racism initiatives in schools fail to gain continued momentum is because people find themselves so deep in the theory that they don't know how to apply it in a practical setting. On the other hand, there are people who are simply seeking a "three-step guide" on how to achieve equity without fully understanding the deep and nuanced theory that provides the foundation for those practices.

FREEDOM TEACHING IS A GUIDE, NOT A GPS. There aren't one-size-fits-all solutions to eliminating systemic oppression in schools. This text is not intended to guide you to a specific destination but rather to give you the tools necessary to reflect upon and adjust your practice.

THE TENETS ARE NOT SEQUENTIAL. None of the tenets are more important or hold more weight than the others. Resist the progress trap of feeling like you have to be an expert in one or all of these practices before engaging. Apply the theory and practice that makes the most sense for your situation at the time.

CENTER THE OUTCOME. Define what you want to be true in the end and work toward it by utilizing the principles in this book alongside best practices from the scholarship that has defined anti-racism work in education.

Notes

1. *Oxford English Dictionary*, s.v. "freedom, n., sense I.4.a," July 2023. https://doi.org/10.1093/OED/1087401921.

2. Zindzi Mandela, "Mandela's Daughter Reads Letter Rejecting Conditional Release," Jabulani Stadium, Johannesburg, South Africa, February 10, 1985, 2:09 video, CBS News, https://www.cbsnews.com/video/mandelas-daughter-reads-letter-rejecting-conditional-release.

3. Assata Shakur, *Assata: An Autobiography* (Chicago: Lawrence Hill Books, 2001).

4. Toni Morrison, "Barnard College Commencement Address, 1979," quoted from "Welcome to the Discovering Toni Morrison Digital Princeton University Library Portal," https://dpul.princeton.edu/tonimorrison.

5. Bayard Rustin, from a letter to the children of Cleveland, in response to a city leader's invitation to write a letter for public exhibit designed to help children understand "the magnificent times in which we live," December 3, 1969. Quoted in "Bayard Rustin in His Own Words: 'I Must Resist,'" by Michael Long, HuffPost, updated February 2, 2016, https://www.huffpost.com/entry/bayard-rustin-in-his-own_b_2881057.

6. Gloria Ladson-Billings, *The Dreamkeepers* (San Francisco: Jossey-Bass, 1994).

7. Rita Pierson "Every Child Deserves a Champion," video, 7:35, TED Talks Education, posted May 2013, https://www.ted.com/talks/rita_pierson_every_kid_needs_a_champion?language=en.

Chapter 3
Hope That Is Radical

Content warning: This chapter contains mentions of sexual violence.

The story of Rosa Parks has been told time and time again. There are two main versions of this narrative. The traditional whitewashed version is that Rosa Parks was a tired old seamstress who was too exhausted to relinquish her seat on one of Montgomery's city buses. This narrative of what preceded the Montgomery Bus Boycott is still very common and unfortunately still taught in schools.

Fortunately, many people know that there is more to the story. The expanded narrative of Rosa Parks mentions that she was the secretary of the NAACP. It highlights that the Montgomery Bus Boycott was a planned direct action campaign and that Rosa Parks was chosen to be the martyr for that movement. People who know the depth of the involvement that Rosa Parks had in the Montgomery Bus Boycott scoff at those who rely upon the narrative that she was a tired old seamstress. Why? Because narratives matter.

Rosa Parks and Radical Hope

The whitewashed narrative paints a portrait of a weak and unintentional Rosa Parks. We know that if we teach that version of Rosa Parks to students, we rob them of the lessons to be learned from the full extent of her heroism. What if I were to tell you that even the second version of this narrative, the one that goes beyond the "tired old seamstress" trope, is still a whitewashed narrative? Rarely is the full, true story of Rosa Parks taught in schools.

Rosa Parks's story of activism starts well before she sat on a bus in 1955. It actually starts with a seed that her grandfather planted when she was a young child. He exposed her to the teachings of Marcus Garvey and from a very early age taught her the value of standing up for her rights and her freedom. Mrs. Parks recalled to Douglas Brinkley, "By the time I was six, I was old enough to realize that we were not actually free. The Ku Klux Klan was riding through the black community, burning churches, beating up people, killing people."[1] Rosa Parks grew up determined to fight for more freedom and enfranchisement for Black people, and it is an injustice to her legacy to start her story in 1955.

Rosa Parks joined the Montgomery chapter of the NAACP in 1943 as its secretary. In this capacity she helped the organization investigate cases involving police brutality, sexual violence, lynching, and other forms of discrimination. While the work she did in 1955 with the Montgomery Bus Boycott is what she is remembered for, there is no bus boycott without her activism leading up to that. Most people don't know that in 1944, 11 years before the Montgomery Bus Boycott, Rosa Parks was at the center of another case. E. D. Nixon, civil rights leader and president of the Alabama chapter of the NAACP, sent her to Abbeville, Alabama, to investigate the rape of Recy Taylor.[2] Many heroic stories about Black women are erased from the history books, especially the stories of those who stood up against sexual violence. Trying to convict white men of rape in small Alabama towns was dangerous business. Not only did Rosa Parks fight for justice on behalf of Recy Taylor, but she also created an organization called the Committee for Equal Justice. She would spend the next decade building her organization, establishing chapters in New York, Denver, Chicago, and Detroit. Her legacy as an anti-rape activist is practically omitted from her story. Leveraging her reputation as an established activist and the network that she built, Rosa Parks helped to found the Montgomery Improvement Association. A young, up-and-coming minister, Dr. Martin Luther King Jr., was then placed in charge of it.

Most people don't know that the Montgomery Bus Boycott lasted 382 days. I think often about what it would have been like to participate in a movement for that long in a hostile environment. To walk day in and day out with no assurance that things would change. I reflect on what it might have felt like on day 20 when you heard stories of people being fired from their jobs for participating in the boycott. I wonder if I would have had the hope to continue on day 100 after hearing stories about people being brutalized on the way home. I think about the arguments that took place in households with one partner wanting to support the boycott and the other partner worried about the family's safety or finances. I think a lot about day 365, which on one hand is a joyous occasion because for an entire year upward of 50,000 Black residents have worked in solidarity toward a common goal. On the other hand I think about the despair that this dubious anniversary must have inspired. An entire year of activism fighting for the most basic right, to sit in the front of the bus, had not pushed the city to budge.

I think a lot of us as educators live on day 365. We have fought and toiled for change and we are tired because we have not seen the change we seek come to fruition. We have hoped, we have doubted, we have persevered, and yet here we are feeling like maybe, just maybe, the change we seek will be right outside of our reach. It took some radical hope to get up on day 366 and stare down what felt like it could be an eternal struggle for freedom. When I tell this story I always think about how powerful a message it would be to say to each of you reading this to hold out for your day 382. There is no way for the folks feeling like they had seen no progress in a year to know that the justice that they sought was near; they just had to keep fighting and believing in it. There are some battles in life that we just cannot afford to lose, and when you take failure off of the table miraculous things can happen.

Instead of telling you to hold out for your day 382, I want to focus on the 11 years before that. There is no way that Rosa Parks knew in 1944 while she fought for justice on behalf of Recy Taylor that 11 years later she would be sitting at the center of one of the most critical civil rights campaigns in the history of the world. I think back to years before that, when Rosa Parks describes in an autobiographical account picking up a brick as a child to defend herself from a white boy. How do you have hope that you can change a system that literally has the license to kill you with no consequence? To me, Rosa Parks embodies radical hope. From childhood on she perfected her pursuit of freedom and justice, not just for herself but for everyone. From her activism in the committee for equal justice to her leadership in the Montgomery Bus Boycott and beyond, Rosa never gave up even in the face of unimaginable obstacles and opposition.

Fixing our education system is going to require this type of hope. It will also require us to understand that the work we are doing now might not bear the fruit we want for another 11 years, or another 382 days after that, but it doesn't mean that it is not important. If Rosa Parks had given up hope in 1944, who knows what would be true about the world today. The reason I choose to hope radically in the face of an education system that has failed the same groups of students over and over and over again is because to do anything else would be to accept the status quo. If I love my students the way I say that I do, if I care about their lives and the world that they grow up in, then winning this battle for freedom and equity in schools is the only choice I have. I am not suggesting that doubt will not creep into your consciousness. I am not suggesting that change will be linear or swift. I am simply suggesting that radical hope is the bridge over even the most troubled waters. Let's practice building this bridge together.

Reclaiming Radical

To revolutionize means to change radically or fundamentally. We are socialized to fear the word "radical." We typically think of a radical person as a person who is "unhinged" or disconnected from reality. As it pertains to systems change, radical is defined in the *Oxford English Dictionary* as "relating to or affecting the fundamental nature of something; far reaching or thorough."[3] Synonyms include *thorough, complete, entire, comprehensive, profound, wide-ranging, extensive.* Some antonyms are *superficial, reactionary, moderate,* or *conventional.* Those of us who want to create an education system that works equitably for all children are taunted with the word "radical" and are often pressured to disassociate from it. In reality the systems that we face, systems of oppression, are by definition radical. They have proven to be so thorough, so complete, so comprehensive that their impact has spread over generations. Even a cursory look over the data tells you just how wide ranging and extensive systemic oppression is in our schools.

Fighting a radical system requires a radical response; anything short of that has proven to be and will continue to be insufficient. As a profession, we have talked about education "reform" for many decades. We have worked to "reform" a system to fit the needs of all children that was fundamentally designed to exclude many of the groups of students who still struggle today.

Let's think of some of the most "radical" reforms to education in the United States. In 1954 as a result of the *Brown v. Board of Education* decision, Black children were permitted to attend school with white children. One could make a very convincing argument that school integration was the single most "radical" reform to our educational system. However, when we examine the impact of the *Brown* decision, we should seriously question whether this reform was complete, comprehensive, wide-ranging, or expansive. The *Brown v. Board* ruling centers on students and not on teachers. As a result of this, the ruling neglected to provide guidelines on how to accomplish the integration that it was mandating. This of course led to Black children being forced to face violent, angry mobs of white parents and students, simply so they could go to school.

Without there being a plan to integrate teachers, Black teachers and administrators were fired in droves. In their essay *Missing Teachers, Impaired Communities*, Mildred Hudson and Barbara Holmes outline the direct impact of the *Brown* decision on Black educators. They state,

> *"In 1954, the year of the Supreme Court's decision in Brown v. Board of Education of Topeka, Kansas, approximately 82,000 African American teachers were responsible for the education of the nation's two million African American public school students. A decade later, over 38,000 Black teachers and administrators had lost their positions in 17 southern and border states. Between 1975 and 1985, the number of students majoring in education declined by 66% and another 21,515 Black teachers lost their jobs between 1984 and 1989."[4]*

A critical review of state after state shows that in the decades following the *Brown* decision, Black teachers and administrators were systematically targeted, in many cases humiliated, and tossed out of the profession. Twenty short years after *Brown,* the Supreme Court took up the *Milliken v. Bradley* case, which effectively decided that school districts could not be redrawn as a means to combat segregation. In response to the decision Thurgood Marshall, the first Black Supreme Court justice and one of the lawyers who argued on behalf of *Brown*, said, "after 20 years of small, often difficult steps toward [integration], the Court today takes a giant step backwards."[5] It took over a century of activism to realize the *Brown v. Board* decision, yet in two short decades the activism of disgruntled white parents were able to pull the few teeth that the *Brown* decision had. Today, schools are more segregated than they were in the 1970s. A groundbreaking decision that had the potential to radically reimagine our educational system in a way that included all children was in reality far more moderate, superficial, and reactionary than many would like to admit.

Did universities evaluate and reform patriarchal systems before the "radical" reform of allowing women to attend institutions of higher education? We could go down the line, from the creation of pre-K without making it universally accessible to all kids, to the addition of feeding students in school while maintaining systems in certain districts in which children can go into debt to eat. Even the introduction of grading systems and standardized tests seems to fall short of the literal definition of "radical" reform. We have a penchant in education for engaging in reforms that are more superficial than they are revolutionary, and because of this it becomes increasingly difficult to imagine real, substantive change. This is why radical hope is so critical if our work ahead is to be realized. We often lose the battle before it even begins because we have been conditioned to champion moderate and reactionary changes that leave the oppressive subtext of our systems intact. Furthermore, we are conditioned to believe that complete, comprehensive, and wide-reaching change is impossible.

In this perpetual paralysis of cynicism is where intersectional systemic racism thrives. Our inability to dream beyond our present circumstance is what allows us to remain complacent in the face of our failure to educate all students. Scholars like Gloria Ladson-Billings, bell hooks, Django Paris, Geneva Gay, Tara J. Yosso, and many others have provided us with a roadmap for revolutionary educational change. The problem isn't solely the tools that we have at our disposal; it is our inability to use them effectively.

If your school has recently hired an organization like Overcoming Racism to come in and lead professional development on culturally relevant and sustaining practices, created a book club, or even begun to shift policy, ask yourself if those changes have been conservative or progressive, reactionary or proactive. How can we assess the success of our culturally responsive interventions if students are only operating in them sporadically? Do we believe that our students deserve to be in anti-racist environments 10% of the time? 20%? 50%? What percentage of racist policy is it okay for a student of color to have to navigate on a daily basis? I would imagine that the answer to that question in an ideal world would be 0% but we know that is not the case.

Perhaps the real question should be, what percentage of racist/oppressive policies are *we* comfortable with students existing in on a daily basis? Is the answer truly still zero? In my work with schools, one of the most difficult barriers to dismantle is the barrier of performative change. A school eliminates a racist policy but doesn't replace it with an anti-racist one. A teacher changes the names on their word problems to be culturally affirming but doesn't shift their pedagogical approach in the classroom. A school district undergoes anti-racism training but does little to shift the policies that incubate racism. When change is superficial rather than complete, the very changes that we are championing can actually just reaffirm the status quo. So if we are going to invest the time, energy, and resources to freedom teach, we have to be committed to doing it all the way. If we are going to be committed to doing it all the way, we first have to train ourselves to believe in and hope radically for change. The "learning to hope radically" step cannot be understated or skipped. While hope might be intangible, the material impact of that hope is substantial and concrete.

Using Our Tools

Radical hope means making our hope for change and for a better future complete for our students. This type of hope usually does not come naturally to us, even for those of us who are optimists. Standing up to systems can make you feel small. Change is often slow moving, it is rarely linear, and typically you have to go through a person or structure that holds more power than you do as an individual. This means that we need to use the tools that are at our disposal and lean into the structures and frameworks that have driven change in the past. One of the first significant roadblocks to shifting systems is a lack of critical awareness of the systems that we are facing. Structural inequality thrives when those of us who have the desire to promote justice are unaware of the inner workings of the systems we are working to dismantle.

Hope begins to falter when our brains cannot imagine alternatives to the systems that we are currently operating in. I was having a conversation about freedom with a friend of mine in which they notified me that freedom to them was paying off their student loans. I can completely understand and respect that personal definition of freedom. However, it causes me to think about why we live in a society, especially in the United States, in which some students can afford college without taking on crippling debt and others cannot. If freedom is being free from debt then there are many students, based solely on the wealth of the families they are born into, who are born free. Other students, by that definition, would be born unfree due to the same circumstances. We either get comfortable in, or feel resigned to, exist in a society in which some people are born privileged and others are not. This impacts how we view the world and often limits what we believe is possible. Just beyond my friend's valid, personal idea of freedom is a version of freedom in which we don't ask 18-year-olds to place themselves in debt in order to get an education.

What we are really talking about here is the development of critical consciousness, or understanding our society and the rules and systems that govern it. We will discuss the research-based benefits of promoting critical consciousness in students later in the book. For now, let's reflect on how we can use critical consciousness as a tool to promote the development of radical hope. According to educator Paolo Freire, there are three steps involved in developing critical consciousness:

- **Critical Awareness:** Becoming aware of the systems that have been set up to create and sustain unequal access and maintain disparities in access to power between groups
- **Critical Agency:** Becoming aware of our power and ability to shift systems and institutions
- **Critical Action:** Taking intentional action aimed at dismantling oppressive structures[6]

I've mostly seen this framework expressed as a linear concept in which people progress from one step to next. I believe that it is more helpful to envision this framework as a cycle because in practice we likely flow through each of the steps depending upon where we are in our personal journey. Think back to the summer of 2020 after the tragic murder of George Floyd. For many white people in the United States that was their awakening moment, the moment they were thrust into consciousness that our system of policing systematically disenfranchised Black people. Of course, Black people have been rallying against racial injustice in policing since the advent of modern policing in this country. However, for white people whose privilege allowed them to remain unaware, 2020 was a breaking point of sorts. This is a good example of a person entering the beginning stages of their critical awareness. It is also a good illustration of why this framework better serves us as a cycle. For a few months the people who were thrust into their awareness purchased books, attended protests, and even placed signs in their yards. For a little while there was a feeling of collective agreement that we needed significant reform in policing in this country.

However, I believe it is safe to assert that this momentum was not sustained. For many of the people thrust into critical awareness as a consequence of the murder of George Floyd, there was no clear mechanism for them to develop their agency and inform their actions based on their belief that they had the power to make change. As a result, they left the battlefield. Those who have been working through this cycle over the course of their lifetime remain to face the predictable racist backlash to calls for change. Typically this just reinforces in the minds of those who are new to anti-oppression work that their effort is futile. For those who don't continue their journey through the cycle, their effort is not futile; it is simply incomplete. It is important to note that you might be in the critical action phase of your journey and have a clear plan on what you need to do to make change. You might be in the critical action phase of your journey and don't know what to do but you are still taking action and moving your work forward. As long as you continue to develop your awareness and embrace your agency to make change, you are doing the work.

It is not uncommon to feel hopeless in the face of the immensity of the challenge that we have ahead of us. That feeling of hopelessness steals our joy and our energy to continue our work. The source of that hopelessness is often misattributed to this nagging notion that revolutionary change is impossible. It is not impossible; it is just that we often stop before we see our work through to completion. Once we are aware of the systems that we want to change and how they operate, develop the belief in our agency to make change, and act collectively on that belief, our radical hope will be rewarded.

Let me be clear: there are days that I wake up and I feel hopeless. It seems like there are weekly reminders that powerful people often use their power to shore up oppressive systems rather than dismantle them. On those days I remind myself that we will win this battle for justice and equity. Why am I so sure of this? Well, if we truly love our students and care about them and their future the way that I know you do, then winning this battle for equity and justice is the only choice we have. When we remove the option of failure because we know that our students are on the line, that shifts the urgency of our work.

Notes

1. Douglas Brinkley, *Rosa Parks: A Life* (New York: Penguin Books, 2005).

2. Danielle McGuire, *At the Dark End of the Street: Black Women, Rape, and Resistance: A New History of the Civil Rights Movement from Rosa Parks to the Rise of Black Power* (New York: Alfred A. Knopf, 2010).

3. *Oxford English Dictionary*, s.v. "radical, adj., sense 1.a," July 2023. https://doi.org/10.1093/OED/4861001929.

4. Mildred J. Hudson and Barbara J. Holmes, "Missing Teachers, Impaired Communities: The Unanticipated Consequences of *Brown v. Board of Education* on the African American Teaching Force at the Precollegiate Level," *Journal of Negro Education* 63, no. 3 (1994): 388–93, https://doi.org/10.2307/2967189.

5. Thurgood Marshall, *Milliken v. Bradley*, 418 U.S. 717 (1974).

6. Paulo Freire, *Education for Critical Consciousness* (New York: Seabury Press, 1973).

Chapter 4

From Radical Hope to Practice

In the essay "Changing the Discourse in Schools," Eugene Eubanks, Ralph Parish, and Dianne Smith assert that "schools are a major part of society's institutional processes for maintaining a relatively stable system of inequality."[1] They go on to outline how the universal acceptance of a dominant set of norms creates an illusion of equality. The general belief is that if students can assimilate to the set of norms valued in schools, they will succeed. Students who struggle to assimilate to those dominant sets of rules will fail. This calculation means that a student's success and/or failure is completely in their own hands. This underlying assumption is why programs that promote "grit," overemphasize behavior correction, and punish students harshly when they fall outside of the boundaries of those norms are so popular in urban school settings. What is interesting, though, is that when you change the demographic of students, these same messages are rarely centered in independent schools that serve predominantly white and wealthy children.

Of course, we want students to be personally accountable for their actions. We want to create environments where hard work and dedication are rewarded with success and acceptance. The problem is that there is often an assumption that students struggle because they refuse to hold themselves accountable. Instead, we should be asking ourselves whether the systems we have placed them in serve them equitably if they do. Some of the students I had the most difficult time teaching also consequently were the students who were the most critically aware that they would be held accountable for their actions both inside and outside of school. The issue wasn't that they weren't accountable for their actions; it was often that they didn't see how their compliance with the dominant set of norms at schools changed the material conditions of their life.

Pedro Noguera talks about the "social contract" that governs schools (Figure 4.1). He writes that "an implicit social contract serves as the basis for maintaining order in schools as it does in society: in exchange for an education, students are expected to obey the rules and norms within a school."[2] Simply put, we ask students to relinquish their basic rights and freedoms, and in exchange for their compliance we promise them an education.

This seems like an exceedingly fair trade, especially when you consider that students are often promised that an education is a panacea for all types of problems. We tell students that being more educated means that they will get a better job, make more money, break generational curses—the list goes on. The messaging for students is basically *Sit down, be quiet, do your work and your education will take care of the rest.* We tell students that education is like a passport. Once they have attained it, it will allow them to travel with ease through the spaces that they need to navigate in order to attain success. We tell students that an education means easier access to jobs, more happiness, and wealth, and in some cases the data determines this to be true. We even go as far as telling some students that an education is a singular pathway to breaking generational curses, undoing poverty, and disrupting patterns of trauma. Students should sit down, listen, and learn because in our hands as educators we possess the key to their future. Obviously success in the real world is much more complicated than that. A strong education is a critical tool that we want our students to have, but it is one of many tools that they will need to author their collective liberation. The reality is that most students buy into the social contract; if they didn't, schools couldn't

**STUDENTS
EXCHANGE
COMPLIANCE**
(Basic rights and
freedoms)

THE

**GROUPS OF
STUDENTS THE
SOCIAL
CONTRACT
FREQUENTLY
FAILS**

- STUDENTS WHO
  STRUGGLE
  ACADEMICALLY

- STUDENTS
  FROM
  MARGINALIZED
  BACKGROUNDS

- STUDENTS WHO
  DEAL WITH
  TRAUMA

- STUDENTS
  WITH SPECIAL
  NEEDS

- STUDENTS WHO
  ARE TAUGHT BY
  INEXPERIENCED
  TEACHERS

- STUDENTS WHO
  FEEL THEIR
  LEARNING IN
  SCHOOL ISN'T
  RELEVANT TO
  THEIR LIVED
  EXPERIENCE

(THIS WORKS
FOR MOST
KIDS)

**BASIC
SOCIAL
CONTRACT
IN SCHOOLS**

**GROUPS OF
STUDENTS WHO
ARE MOST
FREQUENTLY
PUNISHED IN
SCHOOLS**

- STUDENTS WHO
  STRUGGLE
  ACADEMICALLY

- STUDENTS
  FROM
  MARGINALIZED
  BACKGROUNDS

- STUDENTS WHO
  DEAL WITH
  TRAUMA

- STUDENTS
  WITH SPECIAL
  NEEDS

- STUDENTS WHO
  ARE TAUGHT BY
  INEXPERIENCED
  TEACHERS

- STUDENTS WHO
  FEEL THEIR
  LEARNING IN
  SCHOOL ISN'T
  RELEVANT TO
  THEIR LIVED
  EXPERIENCE

**STUDENTS
RECEIVE
LEARNING &
EDUCATION**
(With the promise of - better employment
options, better health outcomes, better family
outcomes, etc...)

Figure 4.1 The basic social contract in schools.

Infographic by Overcoming Racism LLC. Adapted from the work of Pedro A. Noguera, including "What Discipline Is For: Connecting Students to the Benefits of Learning," in *Everyday Antiracism: Getting Real about Race in Schools*, ed. M. Pollock (New York: New Press, 2008, pp. 132–37).

function. All of the power that we have as adults in schools is ceded to us by the students.

Pedro Noguera goes on to talk about the students whom the social contract serves the least; those are the groups of students who don't receive their end of the bargain even when they show up and give their compliance. Black, Brown, and Indigenous students, students who experience trauma, students who live in poverty, students in the LGBTQIA+ community, students who have special needs, students who are taught by the most inexperienced teachers, students who struggle academically, and as mentioned above, students who don't see the relevance between what they learn in school and their real-life material needs. Of course, this is not an exhaustive list, but I am sure you get the point. I have worked with students who were behind academically even though they were the hardest workers in my class, stayed late to put in extra time after school in tutoring, and still didn't leave my school having fully realized the education that we promised them.

We live in a culture in which we will pay annual fees to ensure our packages come in two days, yet with a serious face we will tell a kindergartener that if they work hard for the next 13 years they will go to this magical place called college. Our students need to feel like their education is relevant to their lived experiences now, because the needs of many of the students whom the education system fails are much more proximate than others. I can travel and speak in front of any school district in the country, and give this same list of students that the social contract fails. I have yet to find a district or network to tell me "not here." What this means is that we know the groups of students who our social contract is failing. This knowledge should provide the foundation for us either to amend the social contract or to create a new one that serves all kids. Instead I just change the title on the slide to "groups of students who face the most discipline in schools" and run off the same list.

As stated earlier in the book, the reason we can fix these broken systems is because these are not passive realities. We have made the choice to punish the children whom the social contract fails instead of redefining the social contract. If we know the groups of students whom the social contract fails, then we should also be ahead of the task of making sure it works for all students. For the most part, without even knowing what is going on in your school, your district, or your network, if we pulled the data, chances are we would find some disparities that adversely affect the aforementioned student groups. What that tells me is that we know—or at least we can find—the groups of students for whom the social contract is failing. This should make our job easier; all we need to do is to isolate what is going wrong for these students and fix it. Easier said than done, I know, but the real question is are we really trying? Not trying in the sense that we are throwing things at the wall and hope that they stick. I mean really trying, as in creating strategies that target these groups of students and measuring our progress, with the belief that, if these disparities are maintained, that is evidence that there is something wrong with our approach, not something wrong with the students. We know the students for whom the social contract is failing; it should not be a mystery to any of us. So instead of working to fix the students, who are not broken, we should be focusing on ensuring that this social contract works for all students. If we recognize that we are educating our students in a system in which many of them do not have the power, then it is our job to create schools that empower students while they are in our care.

Sharing Power with Students

We are educating many of our students in a social reality in which they do not have the power. Pause and think for a moment about common human reactions to feeling powerless. What I most frequently hear in my workshops is that people that feel powerless often act out, give up, despair, or take their lack of power out on another person who they perceive has less power (bullying). I remind them that there are positive things too: they may organize, rebel, work to change the power system, and so on. Either way, most of these natural human behaviors are penalized in schools. Rather than changing the context that students exist in so that school is a place in which they feel powerful, we often create new and creative systems to respond to the symptoms of powerlessness. If you have ever felt like you are chasing your tail when trying to shift the culture of a school or a classroom, it is likely because this is a vicious cycle. Groups of students feel powerless, they act out in ways that people who feel powerless act out, and we create new rules to adjust for their behavior.

Putting radical hope into practice means we have to shift the context for our students. When we center our students in their education, we empower them. Students who are empowered are more likely to take risks and try hard things. In all that we do, we should aim to make students participants in their educational process rather than passive bystanders. In our work with schools we find that the root of the reason why school leaders and classroom teachers hoard power from students is fear. Intellectually empowered students might question authority rather than taking everything that we ask them to do at face value. Intellectually empowered students might want to know the why behind our decisions rather than submissively agreeing to them. Intellectually empowered students might resist systems and policies that they feel do not serve them. I have seen the fear that students might engage in oppositional behavior outweigh all other logic about what is best for students' growth individually and academically. The harsh reality is that whatever decisions we make out of fear are usually predicated on deficit-based thinking.

If we are going to keep students in restrictive environments because we don't trust them with freedom, then we need to be honest about that. No more "The students have to be silent in the hallway at all times because what if there is a fire drill." Or "The students can't dye their hair or wear culturally appropriate hairstyles because it is a distraction to the learning environment." Or believing that if a student's shirt comes untucked it means that they are somehow less invested in school. Rules, systems, and structures are critical in schools. Students do the best when they are in environments where they feel safe and what is expected of them is consistent and predictable. I will likely mention this more than once in this book because it is just that critical. Lowering expectations for students is almost always a racist intervention rather than an anti-racist intervention. Creating rules and structures that support the ability of students to resist in transformative ways is an anti-racist act. Creating and maintaining systems and structures that require students to comply even when they don't understand rules, believe rules are unfair, or oppressive is the antithesis of anti-racism.

We either have to be honest with students that some of these rules are either because of tradition or because we simply don't trust them enough to share our power the way that students share their power with us. I understand why the term "oppositional behavior" causes teachers to break out in a cold sweat. Little feels worse than losing control of your classroom and watching students lose out on critical instructional time. If we lump all oppositional behavior together we might inadvertently be teaching students that they should be compliant with stated rules and expectations even when those rules and expectations are unjust or unfair. Think about the impact of that messaging for girls, or students of color, or students in the LGBTQIA+ community. Do we really want to send students who belong to marginalized groups into the world with years of socialization telling them to "just follow the rules," even if the rules are unfair? Students in these communities need revolutionaries who fight to impact social justice movements just like they need doctors, barbers, service workers, lawyers, and entrepreneurs. If we stop to think about it, oppositional behavior isn't our enemy. Our enemy is when students engage in forms of oppositional behavior that is destructive or self-defeating.

Tara Yosso's work on cultural wealth reminds us that oppositional behavior can also be transformative. One of the most common reasons that students misbehave is an unmet need. Sometimes students engage in oppositional behavior to communicate that something is not working for them in the classroom. When student misbehavior causes students to miss out on learning or distracts their peers from their learning, that behavior doesn't bring them closer to addressing their unmet needs. Misbehavior may be a form of communication that we do not like, but it is communication nonetheless. As a classroom teacher, once I stopped fighting the students that I struggled with and started listening to them, I began to understand how to meet their needs. This is an example of sharing power with students. Students don't always have the language to communicate what they are experiencing in the moment and at times their communication comes out in ways that disrupts learning. This is why building relationships is so critical.

Relationship building isn't just about students liking you and listening to you when you ask them to do something. I had some of my best relationships with students who struggled the most in my classroom. In those instances there were times when the relationship stabilized the student's behavior in my classroom. However, that relationship didn't keep the student from being removed from the very next class they entered and lose out on key instructional time. I quickly realized that the notion of building relationships to stabilize behavior was mostly a teacher-centered intervention. This led me to work to build deeper relationships with my students, relationships that could endure hardship and difficulty—the type of relationships that we have with people we love. In this way, if a student was struggling in my classroom I could leverage the relationship not simply to get the student to focus or execute tasks more effectively, but I could use the relationship to diagnose what the student was really communicating through their behavior.

I once had a student—I'll call him Amir—who struggled greatly from academic anxiety. We were in the midst of a really good streak of classes where he accepted differentiated work, was actively participating, and generally doing great in my classroom. I was calling home and giving good progress reports; life was good. I had learned that if I set Amir up for success early in the class it helped him to get a rhythm and generally helped him to stay engaged and focused. For a student many teachers would assert "didn't care" about school, I learned from building a relationship with him that not only did he care, but he cared greatly about how his peers viewed him as a learner. Calling on Amir early for questions to which he knew the answer eased his academic anxiety and proved to his peers that he understood the content.

One day in class, when I asked my first question to the class and his hand shot up, I called on another student. I asked my second question and his hand shot up; I called on another student. After the third or fourth question, without warning, Amir demonstrably ripped up his handout and threw it on the ground along with his pencil. This frustrated me. I walked over to his desk and told him to pick up his pencil and ripped up paper. His response was to tell me to "fetch," which shifted my frustration to something close to anger. He blatantly and overtly disrespected and had he not spoken this under his breath he would have embarrassed me as well.

An embarrassed teacher is one of the biggest threats to a student's learning. I took a deep breath and walked to grab Amir another handout. On the way back I remembered that Amir felt validation with early success. Additionally, I noticed that I didn't differentiate the entire handout, only a few questions in the beginning. Amir's outburst had little to do with me or with the content. It had everything to do with his frustration at not understanding the material that was in front of him and anxiety that his peers might recognize that he was behind. My lack of acknowledgment when he knew the answers seemed to trigger him. His decision to rip up the paper and subsequently speak to me in a demeaning manner was not transformative oppositional behavior. On a different day, or if I wasn't focusing so intently on building our relationship, I likely would have punished him and neither of us would have learned from this incident. Because of the relationship that I was developing with this student, I was able to recognize this behavior as communication.

At this point in a situation like this, I have to do three things:

- Get the student to communicate more directly what needs are going unmet.
- Support the student in recognizing that their chosen behavior is counterproductive to meeting those needs.
- Support the student in finding a replacement behavior when facing this particular trigger.

After Amir ripped his paper he was sitting quietly and not disrupting other students, so there was no reason to provide a correction while he was still escalated. Once Amir had a few minutes to calm down, I approached him and asked him to help me understand what I had done to trigger this response. This is often an effective strategy because it gives the student a chance to think about whether their behavior was in alignment with the action that triggered it. He let me know that he felt like he was trying to participate and I was ignoring him. What I viewed as an incidental oversight Amir viewed as an intentional dismissive act. I let him know that I understood why that would make him frustrated and apologized for making him feel that way. I then asked what he hoped his action would accomplish. He let me know that he hadn't thought about it; he was upset and he ripped his paper. At this point I recognized that he ripped his paper to get my attention.

We talked further about better ways that he could garner my attention without disrupting class and without being disrespectful to a teacher who is trying to help him learn. After some brainstorming, we addressed his subsequent comment, he apologized, got up to replace his handout, and began working with the student next to him to catch up on his notes. I think about this interaction often because I initially took his comment to "fetch" personally. It bruised my ego, as the student was attempting to do, and my first inclination was to respond in kind. More times than I can count I made the decision to race to the bottom with students, to escalate students when I knew they were upset, and to punish kids when I felt like they embarrassed me. I can't think of a single instance in which that was the right thing to do, even if it felt right in the moment.

In this scenario I was able to see beyond the split-second poor choice that this student made. I was also able to leverage our relationship to understand that his action wasn't informed by malice but rather the collision of his academic anxiety and his desire to answer questions successfully in front of his peers. School wasn't an easy place for Amir. I can imagine how frustrating it would be not to feel successful over and over again in a place where you spend up to 10 hours a day. So for a combination of reasons, me not calling on him was his breaking point that day. I chose empathy rather than revenge and that made all the difference. Some might say that I let the student "get away" with the disrespect. I believe I was able to use an unfortunate series of choices made by the student to help him brainstorm better ways to communicate his needs. The rest of the year with Amir wasn't perfect, but we never had to have a conversation about respect again.

Sometimes we get so fixated on punishing students for their choices that we forget that misbehavior is an opportunity to teach. If a student gets an answer wrong on an assessment, we recognize that this is an opportunity to reteach and for the student to remaster that objective. When students misbehave, that is also an opportunity to teach students about the replacement behaviors that help them to reclaim their power and push them closer to the outcomes they want.

When we share power with students, it gives them the opportunity to take responsibility over their own education. Too often education is something that is done *to* students rather than something that is done *with* students. Students are young people, but that doesn't mean they should have no autonomy over their education. Especially as students get older and begin to explore their own personal beliefs and value systems, it is critical that we empower them to take ownership over their education.

Students who can self-advocate are better equipped to navigate systems and structures in school and in society. When we view student resistance solely as something to fear we simply work to regulate it. This singular approach further isolates students, especially those for whom the social contract fails. If we shift our cognitive association with resistance from being a stance informed by fear to a stance informed by opportunity, we can shift the way that we respond to student misbehavior. Additionally, this perspective allows us to be proactive in addressing student misbehavior rather than overly relying on reactionary interventions. Schools are perhaps our best bet to incubate societal reforms that seek to enhance the rights and freedoms of targeted groups. We know that the genesis of systemic change is rooted in education. Schools are perhaps our most reliable bet to eradicate systems of oppression but they more frequently function in ways that instead maintain the status quo.

Strategies That Cede Power to Students

Control is an illusion. The more we try to control students, the more we create conditions that will alienate some of them. The goal should be to create classrooms that empower students to take ownership over their learning.

PROMOTE INTELLECTUAL EMPOWERMENT OVER "SMARTS." I commonly hear teachers speaking about students based on their skill level in the classroom. Student A is high skilled, student B is low skilled. Furthermore, school systems typically are set up to reward students who are "smart." I personally believe that all students are "smart." The question is whether we can tap into their intellectual potential. Students whose identity is wrapped up in the notion that they are "smart" might be less likely to take risks in the classroom because of fear that wrong answers might shift a teacher's opinion of them. These students might not ask as many questions, fearing that curiosity might be viewed as ignorance. "Smart" students might rush through assignments as if there is a prize for finishing first. Reflect for a moment on the qualities that you might associate with an intellectually empowered student. Intellectually empowered students are more likely to question their learning for deeper understanding. They ask questions because they want to know how to get to the right answer rather than simply knowing what the right answer is. An intellectually empowered student is more likely to disagree or question authority when appropriate. Intellectually empowered students become lifelong learners, and that is what we want to inspire in our students.

ALLOW STUDENTS TO DISAGREE. We should normalize for our students that it is okay to disagree. We should also support our students in their ability to seek out, provide evidence, and back up their arguments. Creating a classroom culture in which you are the only source of knowledge is like being a personal trainer who just lifts weights in front of their clients. Helping students to practice disagreeing with the teacher and with one another respectfully can cut down on disruptive forms of disagreement in the classroom.

APOLOGIZE TO STUDENTS WHEN YOU ARE WRONG. Normalize apologizing to students when you are wrong. Normalize students apologizing to one another when they cause harm to one another. Recognize that intent and impact are two different things. You might engage in a practice with the sincere commitment to leave a student feeling empowered and the impact of that practice leaves a student feeling disempowered. When our intent and the impact are misaligned it is okay to apologize to students and to model behavior change. If we are asking students to apologize to their peers or us when they make mistakes, we should be prepared to model that same behavior for them.

STUDENTS ARE LEARNERS AND TEACHERS. Students should not be viewed simply as empty vessels waiting for us to fill them with knowledge. Students should be engaged intentionally in the process of knowledge creation in the classroom. Students should see themselves and their classmates as sources of knowledge in a similar way that they see the teacher as a source of knowledge. Students are expected to draw upon prior knowledge in the class-room and make connections using that knowledge to learning objectives. Doing this well takes time and skill. So understand when and where you want to employ constructivism as a strategy. Some objectives might be better suited for more direct instruction but there are still ways to engage students in making meaning of their learning in ways that connect back to their lived experiences.

ASK STUDENTS FOR FEEDBACK. Being receptive to feedback is one of the best ways to grow as an educator. If we are willing to seek out feedback from instructional coaches, peers, parents, and others, we should also be soliciting feedback from students. Learning to give good feedback is a skill that can be taught in the classroom.

TALK TO STUDENTS ABOUT THEIR LIVES OUTSIDE OF SCHOOL. Students have entire lives outside of school. The more we know about our students, the easier it is for us to make meaningful connections with them. When we talk to our students about their life outside of school, we signal to them that we care about them as an entire person and not simply as a student in our classroom. Understanding a student's homelife can help us understand the choices that they make in school and respond to those choices in an appropriate way.

EMPOWER STUDENTS TO MAKE DECISIONS ON RULES, EXPEC-TATIONS, AND POLICIES. The more that students feel like they have ownership over their education, the more invested they will be in it. Whether or not they come out and say it, students want to attend schools that are safe, predictable, and consistent. Students like structure when that structure makes sense to them. Whenever possible, we should include students in decision-making. It is likely that students will react differently to a set of classroom rules that are imposed on them rather than a set of rules that they helped to craft.

LISTEN TO STUDENTS. This one feels intuitive but we should really make it intentional. How often do we set aside time to listen to our students? Of course we make time for questions as long as they push the learning in class, but how often is it that we actually make time to simply listen to students to better understand them individually and collectively?

CONSIDER ALTERNATIVE ASSESSMENT/GRADING SYSTEMS. Successful teachers know that they have to switch up their teaching style and approach throughout the year to keep students engaged. Furthermore, different students learn in different ways, so it's helpful to engage students in lessons informed by multiple different learning modalities. This isn't to suggest that we should completely steer away from traditional assessment. The goal of embracing alternate assessment is to give students assessments that are in alignment with their learning styles—while also exposing students to assessments that might push them out of their comfort zone.

GIVE STUDENTS MEANINGFUL JOBS AND ROLES IN THE CLASSROOM. It is important to remember that the classroom belongs to the students when teachers are at their best; they are facilitating learning rather than being the sole driver of it. Classroom jobs should be about students taking ownership and responsibility over the classroom. As much as possible, students should have meaningful classroom jobs that have a real impact on how the classroom functions. These roles and responsibilities should give students opportunities to lean into their strengths and experience success in the classroom. Jobs can also be a great intervention for students who struggle with sitting still for long periods of time without something to break up the monotony of classroom routines. It is important to be mindful that we are not just giving students jobs to "occupy" them so that they do not distract others. A job that is meaningful and can build that student's self-esteem in the classroom in other areas. Giving a student a job just to keep them "busy" can detract from their learning and lower their self-esteem.

ALLOW STUDENTS TO RETAKE ASSESSMENTS. The purpose of assessment is to understand where students are in relation to the content. Giving students the ability to retake assessments not only gives us a more accurate picture of their learning, it also gives students more power over their grades. If we want students to develop a healthier relationship with assessment, we should treat assessment like a checkpoint on a journey rather than the destination. Giving students opportunities to review material that they missed and to study and perform better reinforces students building strong academic habits.

Rather than looking at power in our classrooms through a scarcity lens, we should consider it through a lens of abundance. One of the reasons teaching is so draining is because so many educators have been told that they are the one and only source of power and authority in the classroom. If you have ever plugged multiple devices into an external charger you know that the more things you have plugged into one power source, the faster it gets drained. Power is something to be shared rather than something to be hoarded. Empowered students are more autonomous and adaptive. Empowered students are typically more empathetic, respectful of others, and open minded. Empowered students tend to be better problem solvers and are more resilient.

When I was a new teacher I felt the pressure to prove my "might" to my students, and it seemed like the tighter I closed my fist, the more students felt alienated and resisted my expectations. At my strongest, most of the baseline functions of my classroom functioned without me. Rather than coming to me with every need or problem, students sought to find ways to figure it out with themselves and their peers. My students were open minded about trying new things and trusted that we were going in the right direction together. If need be I could leave my room, address an issue in the hallway, and my students could continue on without me. When I started to give power to students and relinquished my desire for control, my students became a source of energy rather than a drain on energy. When I was tired, underplanned, under the weather, or otherwise not at my best, my students were able to pick up the slack.

Teaching is like directing a choir. The only way beautiful and harmonious sounds are produced is if we trust our students to carry their part. Too many teachers are killing themselves trying to direct the choir and also sing the solo. I can assure you, like David Ruffin in the *Temptations* movie, "Ain't nobody coming to see you, Otis." Our students are the stars. It is our job to put them in the position to shine.

Notes

1. Eugene Eubanks, Ralph Parish, and Dianne Smith, "Changing the Discourse in Schools," in *Race, Ethnicity, and Multiculturalism: Policy and Practice,* ed. Peter M. Hall (New York: Garland Publishing, 1997), 151.
2. Mika Pollack, *Everyday Antiracism: Getting Real about Race in School* (New York: New Press, 2008), 134.

Chapter 5
Free Minds, Free Kids

Change requires belief. Belief is a tenuous state of being. People who are believers, especially those who believe beyond the status quo, are frequently isolated and ridiculed. While belief and imagination are not synonyms, I like to think there is a direct connection between the two. Believers can imagine a world that is better than the one we are currently living in. Some even harness the power to take a step further and work for that better world to come into existence. The irony is that for every person who imagines systems free of oppression, there are people who imagine the mechanisms that keep us bound to it. Year after year I watch the teachers, principals, and district leaders who push for revolutionary change get shut down and pushed out. Year after year I see new regressive policies being adopted in schools. For this reason I refuse to be shamed for being a believer, for having the will to imagine something that works for all of our children. Furthermore, once we have identified that the systems in which we are currently existing repress the brilliance, creativity, and cultural expression of our students, we have an obligation to adopt something new. One of the principal opponents to progress is the chorus of limiting beliefs that rain down upon us as we try to envision and actualize change. This chapter aims to address those limiting beliefs, some of which come from within, so that we can face them with the same intentionality with which we face our broader priorities.

The Mind Is a Terrible Thing to Waste

First, let's define limiting beliefs. For our purposes, limiting beliefs are thoughts, beliefs, or a state of mind that keeps us from advancing our goals or chasing our dreams. Limiting beliefs can sometimes be rational, reasoned, and backed by data, but often they are realities that we have imposed on ourselves or that we have been placed in. Have you ever gotten into your head about something, only to realize once you actually stepped up to accomplish the task that it wasn't as difficult as you imagined? Have you ever worked with a student you believed was a "lost cause," only to realize that your lack of belief in that student was a catalyst for the students' struggles?

I'll never forget running into the student with whom I perhaps struggled the most in my career some years after he graduated from my middle school. He was accepted into a highly selective arts school, and upon hearing this information, shamefully my first thought was "He will struggle there if he doesn't get his act together." Behind his tough exterior he skillfully hid that he had been sewing since he was a young child. In New Orleans, sewing Mardi Gras Indian costumes is a sacred tradition passed down in families. This student had not only gained an interest in textiles as a result of this but also significant skill. When I ran into this student some years later he was modeling, designing his own clothing line, and succeeding in his academic environment.

Yes, students grow and mature, and with that comes change, but—long story short—the student wasn't the problem; the environment that we had him in was. I can only imagine how it must feel going from classroom to classroom, teacher to teacher, and being exposed to the limiting beliefs of adults. While admitting to ourselves that we either hold or have held limiting beliefs about children is difficult, we cannot shift from them until we face them. Furthermore, how often are we asked to identify and face our limiting beliefs about ourselves and the nature of our work? One of the principal obstacles that we face in our anti-racism work in schools is that even those who want to believe that change is possible often do not.

Here are some common limiting beliefs that I hear in our workshops. Take a moment to reflect on whether you have heard or personally subscribe to any of these. Remember, having a limiting belief doesn't mean you are a bad person or not dedicated to the cause or your students; it means you are human. Living in that limiting belief to the point that it becomes a state of mind is what is unhealthy for ourselves and our movement.

> *"This isn't the real world. We need to prepare students for the real world."*
>
> *"Culturally responsive teaching practices aren't going to raise my test scores."*
>
> *"Restorative approaches let students off the hook when they misbehave."*
>
> *"All of this work that I am doing to make change isn't going to amount to anything."*
>
> *"I do not have enough power. If only I were the principal or a district administrator."*
>
> *"I want to engage parents but I know what is best for their children."*

Sometimes these limiting beliefs are not as clear or as direct as the ones stated above. Take a moment and think about which limiting beliefs have impacted your practice. If we are going to address these beliefs, we first have to grapple with the fact that they are there. Generally being an anti-racist teacher means engaging in constant self-reflection. Not just any self-reflection, but critical self-reflection. Whether we like it or not, all of us are a product of our environment and our circumstances. In the context of the United States we exist in an environment within systems that justify oppression through the sowing of ideas that are racist, sexist, classist, and the like. Regardless of how your identities position you, you have likely been impacted by how these ideas inform the media we consume, the education we receive, and the ways that we engage with one another.

If somehow you have managed to eliminate all of your prejudicial beliefs, please stop reading this book and reach out to me. Perhaps you are the key to the magical cure that we have all been waiting for. But if you're anything like the rest of us, then being a freedom teacher means recognizing and responding to where our prejudicial or limiting beliefs impact how we show up for our students.

Reflecting on our limiting beliefs can be challenging for several reasons. One of the most paramount is that our limiting beliefs often conflict with the person we see ourselves to be. Our consciousness tells us that we believe in all children, that all children can learn and succeed in our classrooms, that all students are deserving of an affirming education. And despite these beliefs, our implicit or explicit actions might be in conflict with our moral compass. How does this happen? Well, it has a lot to do with our socialization.

Limiting Beliefs and the Cycle of Socialization

Bobbie Harro's cycle of socialization (see Figure 5.1) provides a very clear visualization of how people are socialized and resocialized passively unless intentional action is taken to break free.

This framework walks us through how we are first socialized at home by the people we love and trust. From a very early age we begin to receive messages about what it means to exist in our identities. Everything from the toys they play with and the color we paint their rooms, to the clothing they wear and the books we read to them at night, all of these things start to shape a child's identity. We grow up hearing messages in our homes that shape our identity as well. If a young boy falls and scrapes his knee, he may learn at an early age that crying is not a suitable response to experiencing pain. Rather than receiving care or concern for the wound, he might be scolded, "Boys don't cry." A young girl in the same situation might

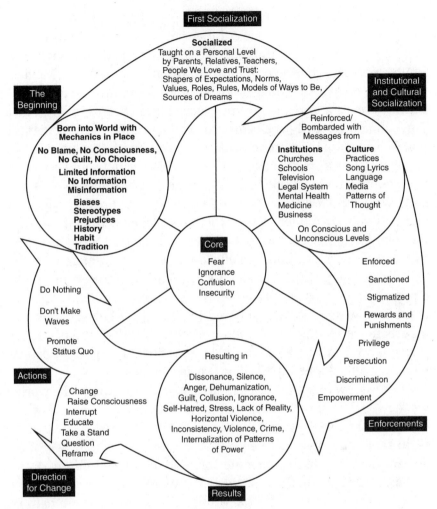

Figure 5.1 The cycle of socialization.

Bobbie Harro, "The Cycle of Socialization," in *Readings in Diversity and Social Justice*, ed. Maurianne Adams et al. (New York: Routledge, 2010), https://www.nea.org/sites/default/files/2021-02/Cycle%20of%20Socialization%20HARRO.pdf

be scolded for roughhousing, playing with the boys, or being unladylike. We receive messages about how our gender is supposed to behave, we receive passive messages about our socioeconomic status, our race, our sexuality, and more.

These messages are then reinforced by both the institutions in which we exist as well as the culture that those institutions create. The child who receives the message that boys don't cry might see similar messages reinforced in the institutions they navigate. Movies, television, music—the imagery confirming dominant views of masculinity are clear. As our collective socialization begins to form, this same child at an early age begins to experience the "enforcements" that keep us stuck in these binary identity boxes. People who fit neatly into the socialized expectations receive benefits and rewards, and people who exist outside of them face consequences. A Black child who speaks fluently in dominant standard English might be told they sound "white." A boy who likes to play with dolls or likes the color pink might be taunted about his sexuality. A girl who excels in sports that are not traditionally correlated with women might be called a "tomboy." Kids who fit outside of the expected norms might face bullying. So as I said before, we learn at a very early age the boxes into which we are supposed to fit and we begin to become experts at perfecting those roles and ensuring that others perfect theirs as well. All types of societal forces push and pull on people who exist outside the mythical box society creates for us.

As we grow older and see a more expansive version of the world, we may begin to understand that the expectations we are trying to live up to are socially constructed and that very few people actually fit in those narrowly defined boxes. Regardless of that, we often assume our place in the machine and hold our own children, or the children we teach, to those same expectations.

I am not suggesting that all forms of socialization are bad. In order to have a functioning society, we have to have some baseline rules and structures that govern how we engage with one another. When those rules and structures are predicated on Eurocentric, patriarchal, heteronormative, upper-middle class values, then by definition large portions of the population will be propped up by those rules and other segments of our society will be cast down by those rules. This is one of the many reasons why it wasn't always my hardest-working students or my "smartest" students who performed the best in school. It was the students who were the most proficient at navigating the culture of school, and in many ways the students who mastered assimilation faster than their peers.

Our socialization is one of the many reasons we put students and their families in boxes. Those limiting beliefs that creep into our heads about the potential of our children have a lot to do with the passive messages we have learned to accept about the population of students we serve. Finding ways to push back against this passive socialization and inform our actions based on the knowledge we have developed for ourselves is critical. This is where the *core* comes in. Refer again to the cycle of socialization in Figure 5.1. At the core you see four words:

Fear: Fear is a paralyzing emotion. Have you ever wanted to speak up about a wrong or injustice that has played out in society, your classroom, or your life, but were too afraid to speak? Fear is what isolates people and makes them afraid of others who are different from who they are. Fear is what tells us that we don't have the agency to change the systems in which we exist. Fear is a very powerful tool in the maintenance of oppressive systems. Fear keeps us from realizing both our individual and our collective power.

Ignorance: What we don't know and don't understand is a major contributor to our complacency within oppressive systems. In our workshops, participants frequently express frustration with knowing that they want to take action but not knowing what actions to take, or simply feeling as if they cannot take action until they are more knowledgeable about the system they are trying to confront. Sometimes our ignorance pushes us to further educate ourselves, but more often it shuts us down. I have found that ignorance is a particularly stubborn obstacle for people who are highly educated. One of the most difficult things about being an anti-racism educator is dealing with the fragility that comes with ignorance. People who are highly educated often do not like to be introduced to ideas and concepts that are difficult for them to understand. It is this fragility that leads school systems to ban books, training, and ideas that make them uncomfortable.

Confusion: Franz Fanon describes cognitive dissonance this way: "Sometimes people hold a core belief that is very strong. When they are presented with evidence that works against that belief, the new evidence cannot be accepted. It would create a feeling that is extremely uncomfortable, called cognitive dissonance. And because it is so important to protect that core belief, they will rationalize, ignore and even deny anything that doesn't fit in with the core belief."[1] Our confusion is often a result of cognitive dissonance. The process of undoing years of passive socialization can be confusing and is rarely linear.

Insecurity: There are several reasons why people might be insecure about taking action against systems of oppression. This insecurity also serves to keep us locked in this passive cycle of socialization. We may feel insecure about the new ideas and perspectives that we have been exposed to. We might be insecure about how our ideas will be heard or understood by our peers or family members.

The results of this cycle are negative feelings for all of us. It doesn't feel good to hold on to prejudices that we could otherwise shed. These negative feelings are what frequently keeps us stuck in the cycle, dreaming of breaking out. If you have ever been frustrated with one of your students for their failure to dream beyond their current circumstances, you can probably look no further than this same destructive core. When a student is acting out from a place of fear, ignorance, confusion, or insecurity, we should be able to empathize with them, because how many times have those same emotions driven our own actions? If we aim to break out of this cycle of socialization then we have to be motivated by emotions that are stronger than the emotions that make up the core. Different emotions may hold more power over you than the ones that hold power over me, but for me fear is the strongest emotion in the core. I have to find an emotion that is bigger than fear to drive my analysis of my socialization and the deconstruction of my limiting beliefs.

Take a moment to write down limiting beliefs that exist around your role as an educator. You can be as broad or as narrow as you want. This can be a reflection on your individual classroom or a reflection on the field of education as a whole. Then take the time to think about where or how you might have been socialized to believe in those limited beliefs. What lived experiences or information did you take in that might inform that belief? Then think about and write down how that belief might have been reinforced over time. The chart seen here gives an example and offers blank spaces for you to fill in your own observations.

Limiting belief	First socialization	Reinforcement
Black students are more difficult to manage.	Statements from parents. Lack of imagery of Black people in school textbooks.	Movies, music, news media.
I cannot teach _____ student because I am not from their community.		

Limiting belief	First socialization	Reinforcement

Take a moment to look at what you have created. Reflect on whether the limiting beliefs actually align with your personal belief system. Think about whether the source that introduced this limiting belief is credible. Now take a moment to think about what has reinforced those beliefs over time. Are those reinforcements credible? What would it reasonably take in order for you to confront the sources of your socialization and the vehicles that reinforced those limiting beliefs in order to be free of them?

Now is probably as good a time as any to remind you that many of the students we serve face very real obstacles. Some of your limiting beliefs might be informed by the very real challenges that many of our students face in navigating the education system or in their personal lives. Some of our limiting beliefs might be nestled in this unfortunate reality. The reason we do this reflection is because regardless of the circumstances that inform the belief, our agency to change outcomes on behalf of our students depends on our ability to first believe that change is possible.

Aligning Our Attitudes and Our Behaviors

Addressing our limiting beliefs is a matter of making sure that our attitudes are in alignment with our behaviors. Holding ourselves accountable and ensuring that our beliefs are in alignment with our practices is critically important. Use Table 5.1 as an example of how to complete Table 5.2.

Table 5.1   Aligning our attitudes and our behaviors: sample.

Values/Attitudes	Actions I Have Taken	Consistency
Students deserve an education that is rooted in their culture and identity. I believe that meritocracy is a myth, etc.	*I plan narrative-aligned lessons. I teach my students about privilege.*	*I use the rubric during teacher coaching meetings once a month.*

Actions I can take, but haven't
I could analyze performance management systems to ensure that success in my school/ organization isn't intrinsically tied to values associated with centering whiteness. . . .

Table 5.2   Aligning our attitudes and our behaviors: template. (You can download blank templates from www.overcomeracism.com/freedomteaching.)

Values/Attitudes	Actions I Have Taken	Consistency

Actions I can take, but haven't

Engaging in this type of activity helps me to visualize whether my beliefs and my actions are in alignment. Whether you are engaging in critical self-reflection because you are dealing with a problem you are trying to solve or you are trying to fine-tune, this activity can have great utility for making adjustments in one's practice. When doing this activity, I have found that I hold several personal beliefs about the education of children that I have not aligned actions with or the actions that are in alignment with that belief I do not practice consistently. I have always prided myself on being a values-aligned teacher, so doing this activity has also made me aware of the fact that my actions have often been more aligned with my strengths than they were with my values. While it is an asset to lean into your strengths, the connection that you need to make with a student might reside in an area in which you need to grow.

Note

1. Franz Fanon, *Black Skin, White Masks* (New York: Grove Press, 1952), 194.

Chapter 6
It Isn't Rigorous, If It Isn't Relevant

Embracing Our Power

It is easy to get complacent while addressing the often critical and urgent symptoms of educational inequality. It is difficult to become the catalyst of change even when you want to. When people see social problems arise there are several reasons why they might find themselves sitting on the sidelines even if they are passionate about the issue at hand. This creates an equity bystander effect where people begin to think that they cannot do anything about a problem or that somebody else is better suited to address that problem. Maybe you are in a new role at a school or you are a first- or second-year teacher and you believe that, because of your lack of experience in that role or that environment, your opinion is less valuable than somebody else's. Or you might be a veteran in your role, burnout might be setting in, and you might feel that some of these problems are better solved by people with fresh perspectives and new ideas. It is easier to focus on why the problem is too big, our power is too small, or why we aren't the ones who should solve this problem. Furthermore, it is also human nature to assume that there is some more qualified person somewhere who is surely working on figuring out these answers, and when they do they will of course let the rest of us know.

When something happens that creates an opportunity to make change, instead of thinking about all the reasons why there might be a person with a skillset better suited than yours to solving that problem, ask yourself what skillsets you have that can contribute to the solution. It is easier to withdraw effort than it is to add effort. White allies often withdraw themselves from this work because they are "afraid to take up space," but in reality people more often sit on the sidelines because they are afraid of correction. If you are truly an ally then you welcome correction, and if you take up space in ways that are harmful then when the correction comes you grow from that. But if you don't contribute in the first place because of this fear, then you only serve to exacerbate the problem.

There is a parable about babies in a river. Different people tell it different ways, but it goes something like this. You and a friend are walking beside a fast-flowing river. It is a nice day outside and the sun is out, but you feel the breeze whistling across the back of your neck. At this moment you don't have a care in the world. All of a sudden your friend shrieks, "Look! There's a baby in that river!" Without thinking you jump into the river, clothing and all. You grab the baby and swim it to shore. You and your friend immediately begin to look around, but you see no parents in sight. Before you have time to catch your breath and wrap your head around what just happened, another baby comes streaming down the river. You pass the baby in your arms to your friend and ask them to dry it off. The baby is cold from its dip in the river. Once again you instinctively jump in to save the next baby from the water. At this point another friend has caught up to you and is puzzled by what is going on. Once you fish that baby out of the water, you immediately notice another baby streaming down the river. You again pass the baby to your friend to dry it off. They pass the baby in their hands to the friend who just arrived and ask them to find the baby some clothes. You fish the next baby out and yet again there is another baby flowing down the river. Luckily another friend has just arrived at the river in the midst of all of this commotion. You pass your baby off to be dried, your friend passes theirs off to be clothed, the next friend passes their baby off to be fed. Imagine this goes on and on in this cycle for some time. At some point your group likely draws the attention of the media, and somebody comes by and captures your heroism and uploads the video to social media.

You are heroes; if not for you and your friends surely these babies would be doomed in this river. The media attention has helped you to build up a team of volunteer divers who take turns fishing out the babies. Eventually you are awarded the Presidential Medal of Freedom for your bravery. One of your friends attracts the attention of some of our country's greatest minds and they invent a series of machines that are perfect for drying off these babies. Your other friend organizes a nonprofit organization that accepts donations of new or slightly used baby clothes in order to clothe all the babies being pulled out of the river. Your sibling receives a significant grant in order to purchase enough food and to pay a team to help feed all these babies. One by one you have all managed to save these children. Due to your sheer will, courage, and determination you have managed to free these babies from their surely doomed condition.

In the midst of all of the attention, the accolades, the donations pouring in, what is the one thing that each of you forgot to ask? Who or what is putting the babies in the water in the first place? Over time we get so used to the unjust conditions in which we are operating that we stop asking how they got so unjust to begin with. Furthermore, sometimes we get so caught up in the process of doing "good" that we don't stop to ask if what we are doing is transformative or if we are just maintaining the status quo. It is also possible to get hooked on the "good" that we are doing. We believe that interventions that might correct the issues we are trying to solve at their source might make us obsolete.

This analogy usually ends here but I have to imagine that there are also people who recognized that the babies should not have been in the river but do not feel that they have the power to do anything about it. Sometimes it just feels more convenient, or feasible, to solve problems downstream than it does to solve them at their source. There is a difference between being aware of a problem and feeling like you have the agency to solve it.

Paulo Friere's cycle of critical consciousness development speaks to this dynamic. Friere lays out three stages of how individuals develop critical consciousness:

- Critical awareness
- Critical agency
- Critical action

The first stage, building critical awareness, entails gaining knowledge about the systems and structures that create and sustain inequality. Many people find themselves stuck here. Being aware of a problem but developing the sense of agency to change the problem can feel even more deflating than ignorance of the problem in totality. This is perhaps why the next stage in the cycle is critical reflection, which means developing a sense of power and capability to change systems and thus life outcomes. Last is critical action, which refers to our ability to take action against oppressive systems.[1]

One of the favorite detractions from doing anti-racism work with children in schools is that if we teach children of color about racism it will fuel a "victim" mentality. It is actually quite the opposite. Helping students to understand that they have the agency to change systems and equipping them with transformative rather than self-defeating actions builds within them the confidence and self-esteem to tackle these problems head on. Students of color don't have the luxury of ignorance when it comes to issues of racial oppression. Many of these students will become forcibly aware of racism as a result of their lived experiences. Educating our students about racism means giving them the knowledge and tools that they need to minimize its impact on their lives.

I understand why people feel threatened by new ideas impacting the way we teach students, especially when those new ideas require us to reimagine and reevaluate our practices. I have personally had to wrestle with the cognitive discomfort of learning that things I did in my classroom in the past were probably harmful for some of my students. Change is not easy. However, staring down the results of the school system generation after generation reveals that change is not only necessary, it is urgent.

One of the biggest obstacles that we have to challenge in Overcoming Racism anti-racism workshops is the mindset of "If I could do it then they should be able to as well." Yes, racism, sexism, classism, and the like are bad, but if I was able to overcome them and make it to college and find success then there are no excuses for my students. It is easy to find oneself falling into this deficit-based mindset that blames children for social conditions and realities that they had no part in authoring. In his foreword to the book *Too Much Schooling, Too Little Education*, Haki R. Madhubuti asserts:

> Black students must have deep understandings of the political, racial, economic, scientific and technological realities that confront the very survival of [Black] people locally, nationally and internationally. . . . Students must possess a deep understanding of the world in which they have to function. However, we do know that the foundation of their knowledge must be anchored in positive self-concept as it pertains to race and identity, and an environment that encourages growth. It is clear that if one is secure in one's self, that which others project—in all areas—will be less appealing, confusing or threatening.[2]

This message is true for all student groups who face oppression. First we recognize that understanding systems of oppression is a matter of survival. We would be judged as immeasurably cruel if we didn't offer students food in school, or if we removed all of the water fountains, because food and water are matters of survival. We should judge ourselves harshly if we aren't being intentional about how we teach students to navigate systems of oppression. Imagine if you had a young child and you realize there is a poison ivy plant in your backyard. What steps might you take to keep your child safe? You would likely first try to remove the plant. If somehow you were unsuccessful in that effort then I imagine the next step would be to obstruct the plant in some way. If all else fails you would of course work to teach your child to identify the plant so they could avoid interacting with it. Systemic racism is far more dangerous than a poison ivy plant. Yet our school systems are often left unequipped to uproot racism. Even worse, they frequently pretend that it doesn't even exist. This conscious denial of our obligation to solve these persistent problems only ensures that they will continue.

While many of us have been socialized to hold on to individual definitions of freedom, the story at the beginning of the chapter illuminates that freedom is truly defined by how it is shared. I would go as far as to argue that there is no such thing as individual freedom. In this way, freedom teaching is any deliberate action that enhances the freedom of all children. For too long we have existed in an education system that very deliberately enhances the freedom of some children and has served to depress the freedom of others. In the United States, students who are white, middle or upper-middle class, able bodied, and the like exist in a school system designed for them. In the inverse of that, children of color, children in the LGBTQIA+ community, students who are experiencing poverty, and the like exist in school systems designed with contempt for them.

If there is any question about this, look at the rising tide of legislation across this country directly targeting teachers' ability to engage in intentional anti-racism. Look to the states who are codifying white supremacy and heteronormativity into their policies and bylaws at an alarming rate. It is almost as if to say that even the idea that schools might shift toward equity will be faced with a deliberate movement to reinforce the status quo. We expect students in historically excluded groups to succeed in spite of the brokenness in our education system. This is why many educators seeking to radically reimagine our education system roll their eyes when conversations about the "achievement gap" come up. A gap in "achievement" is a predictable outcome if all students are placed in an education system designed to advantage some and target others, especially when the measuring stick of that achievement is defined through Eurocentric norms and expectations.

The Freedom Teaching Model

Freedom teaching is about realigning our practice behind the goal of liberating students and giving them the power to make choices that afford them control over critical aspects of their life. The impact of systemic oppression is vast, which is why we acknowledge it as systemic. We see the impact in the choices people can make about the food they eat, where they are educated, the healthcare they receive, their ability to build economic security, and beyond. At its core, racism and all intersecting forms of oppression limit the ability of people in targeted communities to make the critical choices that give them control over their lives. In this country people of color have had to fight for every basic freedom imaginable.

Because we are often socialized to see the world through our individual lens, it can be difficult for some to recognize that the simple choices that they make daily might not be available to someone else. It is a privilege not to feel like cooking that night and to order takeout instead; not everyone has that choice. Taking the unpaid internship that would provide great experience in your dream field is a choice that everyone doesn't have. Going to the doctor or emailing your primary care provider when you are sick or injured isn't a choice that everyone has. We can say that America is a "free" country all we want, but at some point we have to acknowledge that the ability to choose is required to maximize freedom.

In this country, it was legal for Black people to vote long before voting was a choice that Black people could make. The same is true for eating in restaurants, sitting in the front of buses, and attending integrated schools. Freedom is about having the ability to choose, and choice and power are deeply intertwined. Some people have the power to make choices for other people or to limit the choices that those people are able to make—choices about what books can and cannot be in our classrooms, choices about whose stories can

and cannot be taught, choices about whose identities are acknowl-
edged and whose are not. The more choices that are available to
you, the more power you have. For far too long education has been
about the replication of the status quo. As noted previously, Eugene
Eubanks, Ralph Parish, and Dianne Smith want to "change the discourse in schools":

> Schools are a major part of society's institutional processes
> for maintaining a relatively stable system of inequality.
> They contribute to these results by active acceptance and
> utilization of a dominant set of values, norms and beliefs,
> which, while appearing to offer opportunities to all, actually
> support the success of a privileged minority and hinder the
> efforts and vision of a majority.[3]

Or as Tara J. Yosso puts it, "There is a contradiction in education
wherein schools most often oppress and marginalize while they
maintain the potential to emancipate and empower."[4] We simply no
longer have the luxury to conduct business as usual. People of color
have fought for centuries to have equal access to education in this
country. Educators have fought for generations for a more inclusive
education system, a system that works equitably for all kids. Despite
all of those efforts, in just the past few years we have seen sweeping
legislation aimed at targeting these efforts. If we want what is best
for our students, we simply don't have time to wait or sit on the
sidelines.

Freedom teaching (see Figure 6.1) is about radically reimagin-
ing our schools and centering not just what our students know but
their power to use that knowledge to author their liberation and the
liberation of others.

The Freedom Teaching Model focuses on schools being a vehicle for cognitive empowerment. Cognition is "the mental action or
process of acquiring knowledge and understanding through
thought, experience and the senses."[5] Some relevant synonyms for
"cognition" are discernment, perception, learning, understanding,
comprehension, enlightenment, reasoning, thinking, and insight.

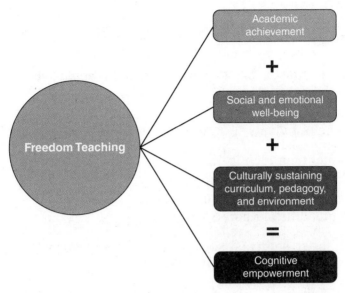

Figure 6.1 The freedom teaching model.
Infographic by Overcoming Racism LLC.

Empowerment is "the process of becoming stronger and more con-
fident, especially in controlling one's life and claiming one's rights."[6]
Instead, focusing on schooling making students "smarter," freedom
teaching already assumes students are smart and capable of learning. Freedom teaching is about promoting cognitive empowerment:
developing students' ability to learn, to think critically, to reason, to
discern, and their freedom to use their intellectual acumen for their
empowerment and the empowerment of their community.

We develop students' cognitive empowerment by creating environments that support students' academic achievement as well as
their social and emotional well-being. Several elements go into
promoting academic achievement and social and emotional well-
being in schools. This is where freedom teaching builds upon and
intersects with so many theories and best practices surrounding
anti-racist education that have come before it, drawing from aboli-
tionist practices, culturally responsive and culturally sustaining
practices, the critically compassionate intellectualism model, and

The Freedom Teaching Model

"Deliberate actions that enhance the freedom of all children."

To help students SUCCEED ACADEMICALLY we need to:

- Center their identity
- Center their academic proficiency
- Center their investment
- Center critical rigor

To foster students' SOCIAL AND EMOTIONAL WELL-BEING we need to:

- Build their self-esteem
- Center their cultural competence
- Center their critical consciousness
- Center their well-being

To help students succeed we need to ensure that their CURRICULUM, PEDAGOGY, AND ENVIRONMENT:

- Are culturally sustaining
- Are community centered
- Are consistent

If we put all that together, we help students achieve COGNITIVE EMPOWERMENT, which is:

- Enhanced student agency
- Enhanced student freedom
- Enhanced student choice

many others. At the bottom of the model you see the inputs of curriculum, pedagogy, and the environment that we cultivate for kids. So much revolutionary potential goes to waste because educators are socialized to see their curriculum as the ceiling or the cap of what they are able to accomplish in their classrooms. More times than not we view the curriculum as the limiting factor keeping us from engaging as anti-racist practitioners. "I would do this but it is outside of the curriculum," "I can't do this because I have to teach the curriculum." If we are going to cultivate cognitively empowered students, we have to see the curriculum as the floor rather than as the ceiling.

We have the power to share our classrooms and to dream and act beyond the limitations of the curriculum. Do we have an obligation to teach the students the things they are mandated by the state, the network, or the district to know? Sure we do. But we have to start viewing that as a baseline rather than the finish line. If the curriculum and the content in the books only create space for our students and their stories in the margins, then we have an obligation to expand what content our students have access to. The same is true for our pedagogical practices and our maintenance of the classroom environment. If we allow ourselves to be defined by our limitations in our knowledge or ability to teach in revolutionary ways, then we will always be confined in our ability to reach all of our students. While we have the ability to grow and learn and get better at our craft, our students don't get the luxury of taking your class at the height of your superpowers. Students get us how we are and we don't have the luxury of waiting until we "have it all figured out" to begin doing the work.

Cognitive Empowerment

So much of teaching and learning has been made to be about students' ability to learn information and regurgitate that information on the test. Students who receive and recall information well are considered to be "smart," and students who don't, for whatever reason, are typically considered not to be smart. Most of the teaching strategies that drive academic achievement as the end goal are really about the transferal of knowledge from teacher to student. Schooling then becomes somewhat of a game, and those who learn the rules of the game and master the game do well in school and those who do not struggle. According to Mwalimu J. Shujaa, schooling is "a process intended to perpetuate and maintain the society's existing power relations and the institutional structures that support those arrangements."[7] Almost none of this has to do with a student's true knowledge, intellect, or potential to make a positive impact on society.

Of course, we want our students to do as well as possible academically; this is something that should be emphasized. The reason parents send their children to school is because they want them to learn. The freedom teaching model simply asks the question of why. Why do we want children to achieve academically? Because academic achievement is supposed to be a reliable indicator of a student's cognition. Their ability to acquire knowledge, to perceive, to discern, to be aware, to think, and to reason. Teaching to a test might promote academic achievement if the student scores well on the test and receives a good grade on their report card. It doesn't, however, promote cognition, critical thinking, or problem-solving skills. Paulo Friere says that "liberating education consists in acts of cognition, not transferals of information."[8] A school environment that prepares students both to navigate the normal everyday challenges of life as well as to overcome obstacles informed by injustice must focus on academic achievement being a vehicle to develop students' cognitive skills.

Focusing on cognitive empowerment as our target also opens the door for schools to value and celebrate the skills that students bring to school from their home worlds. Students are coming into our classrooms equipped with the "funds of knowledge" and "cultural wealth" that they bring from home and if we do not have the infrastructure to value and leverage that then it is wasted in school environments. For years the education system has looked at children with immigrant parents for whom English might be their second language through a lens of pity or, worse, contempt. Looking at these same students through the lens of cognitive empowerment, we begin to celebrate how valuable are the skills that emerging bilingual students use daily to process information in two linguistic domains. A student who speaks Spanish at home, speaks English at school, and translates for their parents or grandparents in public spaces is developing their auditory processing, processing speed, attention span, working memory, and long-term memory all at the same time. Looking at our students and their families through a cognitive empowerment perspective makes it far more difficult to rationalize the deficit-based policies that students of color are frequently navigating in schools.

In their book *Raza Studies,* Julio Cammarota and Augustine Romero discuss how "funds of knowledge may include special bartering and trading practices or informal to formal and informal home business and production among a network of households."[9] They go on to describe how leveraging these forms of capital in dominant spaces that are often antagonistic to their survival further illustrates their worth and value. Students and parents of color bring so many skills that go unseen or undervalued. There is a program in Baltimore called B-360 run by a brilliant leader, Brittany Young. Dirt biking plays a significant role in the Black community in Baltimore. If you go farther out in Maryland where the areas are more predominantly white and affluent, there are dirt biking trails and facilities where dirt bikes can be ridden. However, in the inner city the only places to ride a dirt bike are along the sidewalks and the city streets. So what does the city of Baltimore do? They ban dirt biking in the city and even have a dirt bike taskforce and a tip line to "crack down" on dirt bike riding in the city.

Because the city's solution to addressing dirt bike culture in Baltimore was to ban and police it, Brittany Young founded an organization that "lives at the intersection of three lanes; unrecognized potential, dirt bike culture, and STEM education."[10] Using her engineering background she found the intersection between kids who had amazing mechanical skills and interest in dirt bikes and their potential to grow up and become mechanical engineers if they wanted to. I tell this story because it is a great illustration of the oceanwide gap between viewing communities through a deficit-based lens and an asset-based lens. One program, the Baltimore Dirt Bike Taskforce, aims to incarcerate dirt bikers, while B-360 aims to leverage dirt bike culture to liberate and educate. These communities that schools position themselves to "save" kids from come with a wealth of knowledge and leverage if we build relationships with parents, families, and community members.

The other element of cognitive empowerment that we align with academic achievement is social and emotional well-being. When we don't align student well-being on the same tier as their academic achievement, we get education theory and policy that dehumanizes kids. No shortcuts, no-excuses programming, zero-tolerance policies, the overemphasis on exclusionary discipline system all come from an imbalance in our priorities. The desire for students to "achieve" at all costs built up programs and institutions that offered students an education in exchange for their individuality. All of a sudden kids could only learn if their hair was styled a particular way, if they walked a certain way in the hallway, if their socks were a particular color, and if they held their binder in a certain hand. Not to mention how impossible it is to learn if a student's shirt were to come untucked or if a hood was on their head.

Over the last 20-plus years, many urban schools that serve Black and Brown children have become more and more militaristic and regimented based on the underlying belief that if you control even the microdetails of student behavior, that will create an environment in which they can learn. For schools that operate under these ideologies, recess, social time, physical activity, sports, and extracurricular activities are all secondary to time on academic tasks. But if we think about schooling as a vehicle to promote cognitive empowerment, then by definition we cannot value academic achievement in isolation from student social and emotional well-being.

Cognition isn't just about what you learn, how fast you learn it, and how much of that information you retain. Psychologists have identified that cognition is also about your stress levels and how you manage stress. Cognition is impacted by your diet and how much you exercise. Cognition is impacted by how much sleep you get and how rested you are before engaging in mentally taxing tasks. Cognition is even impacted by our social connections and relationships. When scholars talk about "seeing the whole kid," this is what it looks like in practice. This is why it is important to make space for students to talk in school, because students need to focus on developing their listening skills. This is why recess and playtime are a right and not a privilege, because students need to exercise and socialize in schools. This is why sports, enrichment classes, and after-school activities should not be secondary to core academic coursework. It is also why it is important that students are eating and learning about healthy food choices in schools. Our students' social and emotional well-being and their ability to perform well on academic tasks go hand in hand.

It is imperative that we start making the connection between the underachievement in communities of color and the policies that inform their education. For generations people of color have fought for educational environments that protect their mental health and well-being while building their academic identity. Instead, more control, more restriction, more policing, and quite frankly more stress have been put in place in schools that serve Black and Brown students, further aggravating disparities. We see people with privilege and power doubling down on toxic policies that adversely impact children of color. Politicians are banning books, making it illegal for their staff to engage in anti-racism training based on the mere thought that learning about racism might cause white students stress.

Yet when schools engage in best practices aimed at reducing the actual racism that students experience inside and outside of school, these interventions are deemed to be controversial. If we care about the cognition and cognitive empowerment of children of color, then teaching about racism and working to eliminate racism in schools is not optional. A vast majority of the stressors that impacted my students inside and outside of school were tightly interwoven with the intersections of racism and classism, so we talked about them. We became literate about systems of oppression. We asked questions and tried to come up with solutions to the problems that made learning at school harder than it needed to be. Those questions we asked in my classroom led us to examine the food that was in our community, the economic institutions in the community, the housing conditions, and even community relationships with police. My students were in middle school but all of these were things that impacted their lives, so we took time to build a frame of reference for them in my class.

When we are not honest with students about the institution of racism and when we hide their history and cultural contributions from them, we are acting in the furtherance of white supremacy and to the detriment of those kids. As Jarvis Givens puts it in *Fugitive Pedagogy*, "Racial socialization took place in schools and society, whether done explicitly or not. The prevalence of anti-blackness in US popular culture and school content [makes] it necessary to offer purposeful and humanizing perspectives on blackness to support the healthy development of black student identities."[11] If we care about the emotional and social well-being of children of color, then we have no choice but to teach about race. Since 99% of my students in my New Orleans public school were Black, I aimed to teach in a way that separated me from the anti-Black world.

Academic Achievement

When parents and guardians entrust us with their children, they trust us to develop their students' academic ability. We have worked with countless schools and educators who have expressed their desire to engage in culturally responsive or sustaining practices, but they fear that doing so would negatively impact their students' test scores. I don't know of a single anti-racist practice or protocol in schools that isn't aimed at improving academic achievement. If the interventions a school is using don't improve academic performance, they are by definition not anti-racist. We aren't asking schools to engage in culturally affirming practices simply because it is the morally correct thing to do. We are asking schools to engage in culturally affirming practices because they have been proven to create the best conditions for students to learn. This yields a misguided perspective that anti-racist practices center academic achievement because that is something that students of color are missing, rather than connecting students back to a sense of academic belonging that existed before racist policies intervened to disrupt and destroy it.

The dominant discourse in education reinforces notions of educational inferiority by presenting a limited and shallow vision of the academic legacy of communities of color. It was not uncommon in my seventh- and eighth-grade history classroom composed almost exclusively of Black children that many students came to me not knowing that Dr. Martin Luther King Jr. and Abraham Lincoln lived in two different time periods. In the traditional education system, children of color learn their history in vignettes. With anti-racist education being politicized and under attack, it is safe to assume that this reality will get worse before it gets better in many states. It is essential that we leverage students' investment in the intellectual legacy of their communities. Our students come from the rich legacies of their forebearers who have contributed greatly to the academic tapestry of the world. So the message is clear: not only do I believe that you can achieve, but I know that you can achieve because you come from a legacy of achievement, a legacy of intellectualism, and a legacy of cultural wealth.

Freedom teaching centers three key ingredients to promote academic achievement: academic identity, academic proficiency, and critical rigor. This of course does not mean that these are the only indicators, but they give us a common foundation from which to start, as the next sections will explain.

Academic Identity

Academic identity is how students view themselves as academic learners (academic self-concept). It's challenging to develop a strong academic identity if you do not see yourself reflected in the curriculum in the classroom. Growing up Black, kids in my neighborhood tended to align speaking in academic ways or engaging in academic pursuits with "acting white." This comes from years of existing in school systems that align academic achievement with whiteness. Academic identity has everything to do with how students perceive themselves in school and whether they believe they have agency in their academic outcomes. Building students' academic identity means allowing them to see themselves as participants in their education rather than passengers. This is why education is something we should do *with* students rather than something that we do *to* students. The more power students have to teach at school as well as learn and to shape the academic environment that they exist in, the more it will feel like school is something that they are a part of. Too often schools ask children of color to completely divorce their racial and gender identities from their academic identities. We expect these students to adeptly navigate two entirely different worlds instead of working to merge them when and where we can.

Here are some strategies that promote academic identity:

- Centering: Content that centers the narratives and experiences of marginalized groups.
- Pedagogy that counters racist stereotyping.
- Pedagogy that leverages students' cultural wealth.
- Academic rigor: The belief that students can do challenging work—and providing them with the support they need to get it done. Additionally, if the content is not relevant then it is likely not rigorous.
- Authentic caring: Genuine compassion for students improves their chances of succeeding.
- Parent/guardian and community involvement improves students' chances of succeeding.

Academic Proficiency

Academic proficiency refers to actions that develop learners' academic skills or expertise. Simply put, school is a skill. There are students who are labeled as "low learners" or "deficient" when in reality they are simply not as proficient at navigating the school environment as some of their peers. Proficiency is also critical for preparing students to navigate the varying academic environments that they will progress through in the future. This is why cognition is valued over knowledge transference, because skills are transferable. A fear that comes up in our workshops is the fear that students may be learning in a liberating or empowering environment at one school but will likely have to function outside that environment as they progress through their education. This is always funny to me because it is basically like asking, "What if my school is too anti-racist? Shouldn't it be a little more racist so students are prepared for racism elsewhere?"

While I have never been to a school that is "too anti-racist," I can assure you that exposing students to racism in schools as a means to prepare them for racism in society is like preparing for a fire drill by setting the school on fire. By focusing on academic proficiency, we prepare students to function in a diverse array of environments. Cognitive skills like visual and auditory processing, memory, and attention are all transferable skills. Providing students with rigorous reading, writing, and mathematical training are all transferable skills. Teaching students about racism so they can understand what it is and how it functions also helps students to function in dominant spaces.

Here are some strategies that promote academic proficiency:

- Activities that pose problems and promote critical thinking
- Normalizing questioning in the classroom
- Prioritizing students deepening their understanding rather than memorizing facts, figures, or "tricks"
- Connecting what students learn to their funds of knowledge
- Alternate assessments
- Project-based learning
- Constructivist teaching

Critical Rigor

Pretty much every significant teaching model identifies that rigor is a key ingredient for student success. In most of the books that I have read and education seminars I've attended, increasing rigor has almost always had the connotation of making the work that we put in front of students more academically challenging. While this is almost certainly a part of increasing rigor, in most cases it doesn't get to the true meaning of the word. Rigorous means "thorough, exhaustive, and accurate." Our curriculum, our pedagogy, and our assessment of students must be thorough, exhaustive, and accurate. Far too often the end product of increasing rigor is simply putting more challenging work in front of students, but the challenge of the work should be in direct relationship with the thoroughness of our instruction and planning.

Increasing rigor for students inevitably means elevating our teaching practice, and this seems to be the part that goes missing in the "rigor" and "grit" messaging that is so prevalent in schools. This is why in freedom teaching we use the phrase *critical rigor*. The concept of "critical rigor" represents an educational approach that seeks to elevate both students and teachers by raising the level of difficulty in assignments while concurrently enhancing the quality of teaching. It involves setting higher academic expectations for students and equipping them with the necessary support and clear instructions to tackle more demanding and purposeful tasks. Critical rigor goes beyond simply increasing the workload; it emphasizes the development of critical thinking, problem-solving skills, and the application of knowledge in real-world contexts. By fostering an environment where students are encouraged to engage deeply with the subject matter and take ownership of their learning, critical rigor empowers them to become active, analytical, and independent learners.

Simultaneously, teachers play a pivotal role in this process, utilizing innovative teaching methodologies, personalized approaches, and ongoing feedback to guide students through their academic challenges. The symbiotic relationship between increased difficulty and heightened teaching fosters a rich and transformative learning experience, equipping students with the tools they need to thrive both in the classroom as well as in the world. Students should be able to apply the concepts they are learning in class and the tools that we develop alongside them to tackle challenging tasks to real-life problems and situations. In fact, *critical rigor* also means providing students with content that is relevant to their lived experience while drawing upon students' prior knowledge to inform teaching and learning.

To rigor we'll want to add investment, because the two go hand in hand. Students are less likely to engage in rigorous tasks that they are not invested in, and tasks that are rigorous that don't promote investment probably aren't meaningful tasks. The absolute worst thing we can do in the name of anti-racism is to stop challenging our students. While the United States is far from a meritocracy, hard work, focus, and determination are almost essential qualities for people of color who want to have a full array of choices about what they do with their lives.

We push our students to engage in rigorous tasks because we believe that they can do them. Consistently lowering rigor just reinforces external messages of inferiority. The problem is that rigor for rigor's sake can have the same detrimental effect. Having students do things that are hard over and over again without allowing them to experience success is a recipe for disaster. Our kids do hard things all the time; for some of them, just getting to school on a daily basis is hard. Caring for your younger siblings while your parents work is hard. Navigating the devastating effects of institutional oppression is hard. I don't know if I ever taught a kid who *couldn't* do hard things; in fact many of my students had done more hard things by the time they were 13 sitting at one of my desks than I did in my entire lifetime. So I knew that my students could do hard things; it was just my job to get them invested in them.

Building investment meant creating a joyous, determined, and empathetic environment for my students. It also meant getting to know my students' academic needs and differentiating them. The more invested in the content my students were, the more rigorous the content became. For my seventh-grade class after state testing we did a unit on Black Americans in film from 1915 to the present day. This unit drew upon all of the skills that we worked on throughout the year: writing skills, document analysis, reading comprehension, historical thinking skills, and critical consciousness. I developed this unit from a syllabus from a course I took in college. We watched segments of the same films, read passages from the same books, and analyzed those resources in almost the same way. My seventh graders didn't know until the end of the unit that they were engaging in college-level work and beyond college-level theory. Students left that class knowing that the ceiling on their potential was limitless if they were invested in their learning and put in the hard work.

The reality is that school is not always going to be fun or interesting. A part of becoming proficient at school is sustaining attention even when you feel like what you are doing is boring. I tried to make my class as interesting as possible but some days we had to engage in meticulous document analysis in all classes or edit and rewrite papers. I let students know upfront that there were some days where class might feel boring or tedious. By the time we got to those boring and tedious days, my students were already invested in the larger vision of the class: what we were aiming to accomplish and who we were doing it for. In my class we set goals for ourselves and each other. Students managed the accountability systems in class and supported each other in supporting those goals. We talked about and learned about our history and systems of oppression and students connected their success to overcoming those barriers as well. My organization's name is "Overcoming Racism" because the first class-wide motto that my class adopted was "overcome." My students were invested in being overcomers, not just for themselves, but for the betterment of their communities. We created a class-room identity based on something that was bigger than us. As a result of that, when the assignments got hard—or perhaps worse, boring or uninteresting—we found ways to persevere.

In my work in schools I have seen the conflation of lowering expectations with anti-racism. It cannot be stressed enough that lowering expectations for Black and Brown children is almost always a racist intervention rather than an anti-racist one. Anti-racism doesn't mean not holding students accountable, and it doesn't mean not having rules or systems in place. Anti-racism is about replacing racist systems and expectations with anti-racist ones and that should almost always mean even higher expectations for students. If we are truly removing the unnecessary barriers built by deficit-based systems, then it should expand our students' ability to engage with rigorous tasks. As Gloria Anzaldúa reminds us, "If we have been gagged by theories, we can be loosened by theories and empowered by theories."[12] Schools far too often make changes with good intentions that are informed by the same underlying assumptions as the policies that they are replacing. The theory that we use to reform our practices must be rooted in anti-racist beliefs that are empowering to the children that we serve. One of the most direct ways we can counter racist stereotypes in classrooms and schools is by showing our students that we believe in their ability to meet and exceed high standards.

Social and Emotional Well-Being

As educators, we wear many hats. We are not just teaching students; we are supporting the process of raising them as well. Schools can get academic results without prioritizing the social and emotional well-being of kids, just like companies can get economic results by not prioritizing the well-being of their employees. If the baseline goal of a company is to extract every cent of profit that they can from their workforce, then perhaps social and emotional well-being isn't a priority. If the goal of a school is to chase certain test scores, or funding, even at the expense of students, then perhaps social and emotional well-being are not a priority. If our goal is to educate kids rather than school them, then this is a central priority in direct alignment with promoting academic achievement.

Schools that care about students' social and emotional well-being prioritize building students' self-esteem. For students of color, a large part of this is countering racist stereotypes to which they are exposed outside and unfortunately inside of schools, intentionally building the racial identity of students of color. "What students [do] and [do] not see in their books and on the walls says something about what is valued and worthy of study."[13] The absence of cultural artifacts and pedagogical practices that affirm students of color communicates a strong message about their value in academic spaces. Building students' self-esteem means centering their confidence and self-worth in the systems that govern our schools and classrooms. The Freedom Teaching Model focuses on the following priorities to elevate students' self-esteem and social and emotional well-being.

Cultural Competence

To develop students' cultural competence, we need to build, embrace, and affirm students' cultural identity. Our educational institutions must validate and recognize the cultural worth of the students that we serve. In reality, most schools in the United States, if not all, are already teaching cultural competence. The issue is that schools are usually set up to teach students how to navigate only the dominant culture. Our systems of schooling reinforce patriarchal, hetero-, and cis-normativity, Eurocentric, and middle- and upper-middle-class values. In order for students to survive in academic spaces, they are required to learn Eurocentric patterns of behavior, speech, dress, humor, expectations, and so on. It is critical to remember that we are likely already doing this with our students.

It should not be too much to suggest that if students who exist in those dominant groups get to learn from their cultural center, then students who exist on the margins get to learn from theirs as well. If we are truly working to build an intentionally diverse society, we should be invested in all students learning through their cultural domain as well as cultural domains outside of their own. This is how we build cultural literacy in schools. This is how we build a prepared and engaged diverse society. The United States is only becoming more diverse. A student's ability to understand the cultural norms and contributions of different cultures should be considered a treasured asset. In the future, a student's ability to navigate diverse cultures will be a currency as important as their ability to read, write, and compute well. For students of color this cultural competence also serves the purpose of helping to build racial pride and self-esteem in the face of systems that can chip away at them. Marcus Garvey once said, "A people without knowledge of their past history, origin and culture is like a tree without roots."

Indigenous leaders have compared culture to medicine. I like to think of culture like a blanket: it covers us and keeps us warm. Extended exposure to racism in the education system makes the students of color we serve sick. Far too often for these students, their education is something that is done *to* them rather than something that is done *with* them. When students of color are asked to check their culture at the door and take on a completely different culture in their classrooms, we are asking them to take on the cognitive burden of code switching in tandem with their learning.

Promoting cultural competence in our classroom is one of the greatest tools we can use to level the playing field for our students. It is the difference between swimming along with the current or swimming against the current, like running with the wind at your back versus running against the wind. For many teachers, the prospect of teaching in a culturally competent fashion when they do not belong to the same culture as their students can seem daunting. It is critical to remember that cultivating culturally affirming environments for your students is not just "the right thing to do," it also is a data-backed intervention for improving student achievement. At its core this is just best practice. Like everything else in our profession this takes time, planning, and intentionality, but the payoff in the end far outweighs the work up front. Students who feel culturally affirmed in their classrooms are more likely to feel seen and valued and in turn are more likely to take risks.

Some strategies that promote cultural competence in the classroom are as follows:

- **Culturally relevant curriculum:** Develop and implement a curriculum that includes diverse perspectives, histories, and contributions of different cultures, ensuring students of color see themselves represented in the material: source texts, resources, and materials from diverse cultures and perspectives.

- **Affinity groups and clubs:** Support the formation of groups and clubs that serve as a place of cultural affirmation and safety for students. Teach students basic organization and advocacy skills.
- **Multicultural literature:** Incorporate literature from diverse authors and cultures into reading lists, offering students a chance to explore stories that resonate with their experiences.
- **Address bias and stereotypes:** Engage in open discussions about bias and stereotypes to help students develop critical thinking skills and challenge harmful misconceptions.
- **Student-centered learning:** Center students in their learning by connecting it to prior knowledge. Connect students learning the things that matter to them and their lives. Make connections between what students are learning in their classroom and current events or events taking place in their community.
- **Family and community involvement:** Involve families and communities in the education process. Make families a priority rather than an afterthought. Let families know what their students are going to be learning and source from families ways in which they can support their children throughout the unit.
- **Provide role models and examples:** Highlight the achievements of diverse role models, including professionals, scientists, artists, and leaders, who have succeeded academically and professionally. Fill your room with visual anchors and artifacts of impactful leaders and groups. Invite speakers from the community into the classroom to share their experiences with students.
- **Address microaggressions:** Microaggressions are bound to happen. Empower students to recognize microaggressions and to speak up when they take place. Be proactive in addressing and preventing microaggressions in the classroom and school environment, creating a space where students feel valued and respected.
- **Culturally responsive assessment:** Ensure that assessment methods are culturally fair and sensitive, recognizing diverse learning styles and backgrounds. Teach students about concepts like "stereotype threat," and engage them with techniques that reduce it.

- **Language support:** Promote a multilingual curriculum that does not just center English.
- **Professional development for educators**: Offer training and professional development opportunities for teachers and staff to increase their cultural competence and understanding of the unique needs of students of color and other intersecting identities.
- **Culturally centered rules, norms, and expectations:** Connect rules, norms, and expectations to students' culture and identity. (e.g., concepts like Inlakesh, ubuntu, the Black Panther Children's Pledge).

This is not by any means an exhaustive list. It is always important to take into account the unique circumstances of your school and your student population. Implementing culturally competent practices improves student well-being as well as their sense of belonging in the classroom.

Critical Consciousness

Critical consciousness deals with students' grasp of the social realities that inform their positionality in the world. Oppression is an unfortunate reality of our society. Due to no fault of their own, our students will have to navigate oppressive systems. There is no value in sugarcoating this. For communities of color, preparing our children to function within inequitable institutions has been a generational tradition. Our young people's safety and in some cases their survival depend on and has always depended upon their ability to understand and overcome systemic oppression. The result of students growing older seeing, feeling, and experiencing the consequences of oppression with no academic analysis of the context of oppression is often lowered self-esteem. Instead of seeing the faults in the system and developing the skills and empowerment necessary to navigate them, students will internalize their experiences as faults within themselves. There is something to be said about the cruelty and inhumanity with which groups of color have been treated over the history of this country. From enslavement to medical experimentation, land theft, genocide, lynching, and internment, if you can imagine it, people of color have lived through it in the United States. There is something perhaps even more monstrous about pretending that it did not happen. Forcing our communities to live with the tangible loss and impact of the past as well as the ongoing impact of the racist policies of the present with little to no academic explanation is cruel.

Our students need to know that they have agency in changing outcomes not only for themselves, but also for their communities. You cannot have the agency to change a system that you cannot understand or can't see. My paternal grandfather grew up as a sharecropper. My father attended segregated schools for most of his life. There were Black businesses taken by white banks in his community. He told me stories of Black men being shot while jogging in the community in which he grew up. He wasn't allowed to walk into the front door of the local Dairy Queen to get ice cream. Over the years I have watched my father skillfully navigate racism in his workplace, in the schools my brother and I attended, and in public spaces. One year for Father's Day I flew my dad to New Orleans to attend an Overcoming Racism workshop so he could see what his son was doing. At the workshop, with tears in his eyes, he said, "Systemic racism. It took me 60 years to learn that what I have been experiencing for all of these years is systemic racism."

Schools have an obligation to tell students the truth and to help them make sense of the realities of our society. If we have any hope for the next generation ushering in a society predicated on fairness and equality, we have to tell the truth of how we got here so that the next generation doesn't replicate the mistakes of the past. The idea that critical consciousness promotes victimhood in students is just a racist myth aimed at maintaining the status quo. Understanding your circumstances empowers you with the ability to change those circumstances. If anything promotes victimhood, it is denying students the knowledge of how people like them have persevered and overcome.

Dr. Lerone Bennett Jr. argues that our "freedom and unfreedom are intertwined. The long fought journey of communities of color seeking full unfettered access to white institutions has been just as much about freeing white people from the poison of racial hatred as it has been about enfranchising black communities."[14] Despite advocates for systemic racism arguing that anti-racism is anti-white, you would be hard-pressed to find a single example of a progressive anti-racist policy passed in this country that hasn't also enhanced the freedom of white people—from the integration of schools, businesses, and neighborhoods, to labor movements, to the literal ushering in of democracy via Black freedom movements. Every step of progress communities of color have made in this country has also served to progress people who are white as well. This is true for the inclusion of women in the workplace and educational institutions, and for the passage of marriage equality.

The idea that social progress against oppression somehow handcuffs people in privileged groups is simply a myth. For too long in this country, freedom has been defined by who is free and who is not, rather than recognizing that until all of us are free, none of us are. At what point do we collectively recognize that we are all better off when everyone has an equal playing field from which to chase success? For the people leveraging their privilege and power to resist social progress, at what point do we recognize that this is not about the desire to maintain privilege but instead the desire to reinstate domination? Carefully crafting school systems that work for all students should not be a controversial thing, and doing so will require us to think, act, and engage in anti-racist ways.

Teaching students critical consciousness both prepares them for the world as it is while also teaching them that they have agency to change the world around them. Far too often we teach students that the realities that they are navigating are static and for this reason change is infrequent and long denied. It is imperative that students from marginalized communities understand that they also have agency in reshaping the realities of their lived experiences. It is imperative that we send students off to colleges and workplaces with the ability to both recognize and interrupt patterns of injustice. In the absence of this preparation, it becomes more likely that students will internalize discrimination and racism as the result of a deficit in themselves. Critical consciousness allows students to understand that if they interact with a person or system that discriminates against them, this is more likely the reflection of a deficit in the perpetrator rather than in themselves. Teaching critical consciousness also increases the likelihood that students will persist in environments that were created without them in mind. It increases the likelihood that these students can both advocate for themselves as well as surround themselves with the support needed to navigate these environments.

Teaching critical consciousness means teaching students critical thinking skills. It means promoting questioning in the classroom and allowing students to drill down to the "why" behind certain learning targets, rules, or expectations. This also means providing students with academic content that allows them to grapple with complex concepts that deal with societal realities. It is our job as educators to cultivate students who can be active participants both in society as well as in their communities. The counter movement against teaching critical consciousness in schools aims to maintain social injustice by pretending that it does not exist. This is a tried-and-true strategy that seeks to handcuff educators' ability to develop politically engaged students. When our students' very rights and freedoms hang in the balance, we have a responsibility to push back against repressive movements that undermine our students' ability to advocate for a more just and equitable society. We are educating the next generation of leaders and citizens. It is critical that they are equipped with the skills, ability, and passion to envision and actualize the society that they deserve and desire to live in.

Freedom teaching means empowering students with the knowledge that the social context in which they exist is neither random nor fixed. Freedom teaching calls us to help students examine the root causes of social injustice and to understand the intentionality behind it. A house that has been built can be dismantled, and in this same way students must understand the political, economic, and social foundation upon which they are being educated. I once had a

Black student raise her hand in class and exclaim out loud as a matter of fact, "White people are just smarter than us." The comment caught me off guard, as did the relative acceptance of the statement from the rest of the class. In hindsight the question I asked her in response to this statement was a silly one: "Who told you that?" She stared back at me as if she was reaching deep in her memory to find a response. The question was silly because her comment wasn't about what was told to her; it was about what wasn't. It was about growing up as a young Black girl in a segregated city, attending a segregated school, and spending years in a school system that never validated her worth.

What goes unsaid is as important as what is said, if not more important so. Every day Black and Brown children are entering classrooms that omit the intellectual contributions of people who look like them. For this reason Lerone Bennet Jr. calls Blackness a "challenge" because it interfaces with our education system. He theorizes, "We can see that challenge in its clearest form in the educational field. For blackness raises total questions about the meaning of education in a situation of oppression. And in the light of that challenge we can see clearly that an educator in a situation of oppression is either an oppressor or a liberator."[15] Year after year students are experiencing the long-term effects of racist policy. When no one feels that it is important enough to take the time to explain to these students the history of how things got this way, it reinforces the status quo as normal or correct. The combination of this passive reinforcement with the active reinforcement that often comes through our pedagogy and systems reinforces messages of inferiority for Black and Brown students. Giving students the tools to contextualize their lived experiences allows them to develop a sense of agency.

Substantive Affirmation

When schools are in the early stages of trying to implement culturally affirming and anti-racist practices, they typically start with descriptive affirmation. Descriptive affirmation occurs when a teacher's identity or the content that they teach affirms some element of the students' identity. This is happening when students have teachers who look like them in the classroom or when teachers teach content or display cultural artifacts in the classroom that affirm elements of their students' identity. In short, representation matters.

Descriptive affirmation is critically important but it is not the form of affirmation that most effectively drives students' sense of belonging in schools. Substantive affirmation occurs when teachers' actions align with students' identity and values. The content of the teachers' actions, words, and conduct makes students feel valued because it pertains to their identity. This comes up a lot in our workshops when white teachers express that they feel like they are not equipped to affirm the culture or identity of their students because they don't belong to the same racial group. This limiting belief might alone be enough to stop that teacher from doing the self-work that could help them develop the capacity to substantively affirm their kids.

This same mindset is applied in ways that undermine the hard work of teachers of color. There is often a subtle assumption that the Latinx kids behave better for that teacher because she is Latina or the Black kids behave better for this teacher because he is Black. Yes, the descriptive affirmation of the student and teacher sharing an identity matters, but if you look deeper the best teachers are really going one step further to connect to students' values, their culture, and their identity. Descriptive affirmation depends a lot on a teacher's identity but anyone can substantively affirm their students. So excuses must go out the window and we have to start building relationships with our students and their families in order to understand what they value. If you share some critical identities with students, this process might go more quickly, but it is not impossible for a white teacher to substantively affirm a student of color or a male teacher to affirm a female student. Students who are affirmed at the values level will feel more willing to bring their full selves to the classroom and take academic risks.

Curriculum, Pedagogy, and Environment

The curriculum we teach, the way we teach it, and the environment we create for students in our classrooms is at the bottom of the model—not as a reflection of their importance but because these elements make up the foundation that allows us to accomplish everything above it. No matter where you are situated in education, a lot of things are outside your control. As a teacher I felt that if I became an administrator, I would have the power and agency to trade racist practices that were happening at my school for anti-racist ones. Then I was promoted to the administration and felt like I had even less agency than when I had the ability to just go into my classroom, close my door, and teach the way I wanted to teach. Principals bemoan the influence that their network or district has on how their school is run. District and network leaders often pass the buck to the board or other external stakeholders to explain why they feel that they don't have the agency to change racist systems. One of the prominent things that I have learned from working with schools all over the country is that there is always going to be something telling you that you don't have the power to make the change.

For many of us it starts with the curriculum. It feels like some group of people get together in some undisclosed place and come back with structures and guidelines that you have to adhere to in your classroom. One of the questions that we get asked at Overcoming Racism most frequently is how to be culturally responsive when the curriculum isn't culturally responsive. Or from a pedagogy perspective, how does one teach in anti-racist ways if you have not been directly trained on them or if this isn't something that your district values? We allow that group of people who get together in their undisclosed place who give us the curriculum to dictate what is best for our students. Why? Because we have to, right? Yes and no. This book is not advocating not teaching the content the state wants you to teach. We have an obligation to prepare our students for their tests and our jobs and livelihoods depend upon us delivering results in alignment with the curriculum. What this model is advocating is that we see our curriculum and the pedagogy that we align with it as the floor rather than the ceiling. We have the power to teach beyond what is given to us and to create lessons that impart the baseline knowledge that students need to receive while also teaching lessons that build their self-esteem, investment, identity, and so on.

I taught seventh- and eighth-grade social studies in Louisiana. For the seventh grade I taught US history, which coincidentally ended right after the Civil War. For eighth grade I taught predominantly Louisiana state history. Needless to say the curriculum itself wasn't the most affirming for my 99% African American class. If I taught specifically by the book, my students would have made it to eighth grade without having learned anything about the Black experience other than the fact that Black people were enslaved. I did a lot of things to address this, like focusing on developing my students' historical thinking skills so they could make comparisons between the history that the curriculum dictated they learn and other time periods that shared some of the same themes.

I taught a writing unit at the beginning of the year that prepared them for the writing components of the class that taught about Africa prior to European colonization. One lesson in particular, however, always stands out. My eighth-grade students were going to be tested on the Louisiana Purchase, and there were three main things they needed to know about it. First, Thomas Jefferson was president at the time. Second, the purchase doubled the size of the United States. Third, Thomas Jefferson purchased the land at a huge discount from France and the purchase perhaps saved an otherwise rocky presidency. So that was what the curriculum dictated. Using those three ideas as the floor of my lesson on the Louisiana Purchase, I taught all of my students those things.

I also exposed them to some additional primary and secondary sources for their analysis. In these sources, about the Haitian Revolution and Toussaint Louverture, students could find an alternative story, one about Haitian rebels casting off their yokes of enslavement and defeating what was considered to be the most powerful military in the world at that time, Napoleon's army. These documents mentioned that Jefferson's original intent was to purchase New Orleans, a critical location for the trading of goods and enslaved people. France surprised the United States by hastily offering to sell the entire Louisiana territory. This was in April, but Jefferson doesn't even learn about this offer until July. There are several theories about why France would want to do this but the most likely one is that, after the defeat of his army in Haiti, Napoleon no longer had a need for the territory that was intended to be used as a trade destination for the goods developed in Haiti. Because the Haitians and the Haitian Revolution had so much to do with the purchase of the Louisiana territory but this information was omitted from Louisiana history books, my students got to engage in a thought-provoking analysis of the politics of the time. None of the content they learned about the Haitian Revolution—a story about freedom and overcoming rather than enslavement and control—was ever on the test. But my students always got the Louisiana Purchase questions right because they were so invested in the content.

Maybe at your school or district you do not have the same freedom to take some of the liberties with the content that I did. That doesn't mean there are no other avenues with which to build an environment for kids in your classroom that is anti-racist and culturally affirming. If we focus on what we can't do, we are doomed just to reinforce the status quo. If we instead look at our curriculum as a baseline, then there is a lot of room to get creative about how we teach that curriculum.

I could not accept the idea of my students not learning anything affirming about Blackness in their history classes, perhaps in their life, but at the very least until they made it to high school, no matter who decided what the curriculum was or why they decided to start and stop it when they did. If I was going to build my students' achievement at the same time that I was building their social and emotional well-being, I knew that I had to go above and beyond what was given to me. I had to make choices that got my students closer to the end goal of cognitive empowerment. Those were the choices that had a life-long impact on the kids I served.

Notes

1. Paulo Freire, *Education for Critical Consciousness* (New York: Seabury Press, 1973).

2. Mwalimu J. Shujaa, ed., *Too Much Schooling, Too Little Education: A Paradox of Black Life in White Societies* (Trenton: Africa World Press, 1998), 5.

3. Eugene Eubanks, Ralph Parish, and Dianne Smith, "Changing the Discourse in Schools," in *Race, Ethnicity, and Multiculturalism: Policy and Practice*, ed. Peter M. Hall (New York: Garland Publishing, 1997).

4. Tara J. Yosso, "Whose Culture Has Capital? A Critical Race Theory Discussion of Community Cultural Wealth," *Race Ethnicity and Education* 8, no. 1 (2005): 74.

5. *Oxford English Dictionary*, "cognition."

6. *Oxford English Dictionary*, "empowerment."

7. Shujaa, *Too Much Schooling*, 15.

8. Paulo Freire, *Pedagogy of the Oppressed* (London: Penguin Classics, 2017), 79.

9. Julio Cammarota and Augustine Romero, *Raza Studies: The Public Option for Educational Revolution* (Tucson: University of Arizona Press, 2014), 124.

10. "B-360 exists at the unlikely intersection of three lanes; unrecognized potential, dirt bike culture, and STEM education" (B-360 home page), n.d., https://b360baltimore.org/.

11. Jarvis R. Givens, *Fugitive Pedagogy: Carter G. Woodson and the Art of Black Teaching* (Cambridge, MA: Harvard University Press, 2021), 208.

12. Gloria Anzaldúa, *Making Face, Making Soul/Hacienda Caras: Creative and Critical Perspectives by Women of Color* (San Francisco: Aunt Lute Books, 1990), 26.

13. Givens, *Fugitive Pedagogy*, 203.

14. Lerone Bennett Jr., *The Challenge of Blackness* (Chicago: Johnson Publishing Company, 1972).

15. Ibid., 40.

Chapter 7
Trouble Doesn't Teach

"*It is easier to build strong children than it is to repair broken [adults].*"

—*Frederick Douglass*

Freedom teaching means providing students with a liberatory education. Think about the qualities of a liberated student. This student is likely a critical thinker; they want to know how something works rather than just knowing that it works. A liberated student is curious and unafraid to ask questions. This student is more likely to take risks, more likely to take on leadership, and more likely to take on ownership for the outcomes in their life and their environment.

Anti-racist education practices are usually attached to racist myths. One of the most dangerous of those myths is that these practices promote a victim mindset or lower expectations for student behavior in schools. It cannot be said often enough that any intervention that lowers expectations for students of color is far more likely to be a racist intervention than an anti-racist one. Ceding power to students in their academic environments does the opposite of promoting victimhood. We are actively teaching students—many of whom live in a broader social context in which they do not have power—that they have power at school. We teach them what responsibilities come with that power and the consequences, both positive and negative, that come when that power is wielded ineffectively. The rules that exist in school should exist to provide students with a safe and consistent environment so that they can learn freely and creatively.

Far too often, rules and discipline systems focus instead on exerting control. The thought process is that if students are "under control" then learning will automatically take place. There is also often an investment in the optics of control. Sometimes we become so invested in the aesthetic of quiet hallways and classrooms full of compliant students completing tasks as they are told to do them that we lose sight of the actual goal of school, which is for students to learn. The issue often isn't with the end goal of what we want to see in our classrooms. We want to see students who are engaged; we want classrooms that are as free from unnecessary distractions as possible; we want students and teachers to treat each other with respect. The issue is with how we get there. Synonyms to the word "control" are words like dominance, command, rule, reign, oversight, and authority. As adults, if we were asked if we would do our best work in an environment marked by "domination" or "authority," most of us would disagree. We might want structure, but domination? We might want accountability, but authority? Once we create the standard that students should require to be controlled in order for them to learn, then students will acquiesce to that. However, when it is time to learn outside of the reins of that authority or control, those students will flounder.

I want students to behave in school because they are invested in their education and the education of their peers. I want students to understand that no one can "control" them and if they want to maintain their freedom from controlling environments, they have to learn the skill of self-control. In controlling environments, when students make mistakes, there is an over-emphasis on the trouble that the student gets into at that moment. Student compliance is based solely on the deterrents we pile up in front of them. So students behave because they don't want to get punished. Then as they get older, for some students those punishments begin to carry less and less weight or meaning. The students who need the most behavioral support instead receive the most behavioral control. After years of being in trouble, instead of being taught to make better choices certain students just become more and more disinvested in school.

Students are going to misbehave. They are going to make mistakes and make poor choices from time to time. Any misbehavior that actually warrants an authoritative response is likely a misbehavior that also moves a student further from their goals. My job as a liberatory educator is to help that student recognize replacement behaviors that get them closer to their goals.

Students come to school with great aspirations: to better their lives, to better their families lives, to work toward a desired career or lifestyle, and much more. Trouble doesn't teach students to make transformative choices rather than self-defeating ones. It doesn't help them to understand which choices will bring them closer to their goal of having a greater sense of freedom and the ability to make choices and control critical elements of their lives. Giving students the opportunity to correct their behavior and make better choices humanizes them. It also furthers our goal of putting students in school environments in which they feel powerful instead of powerless.

It should go without saying that anti-racism is not in alignment with a lack of accountability. If anything, anti-racist discipline systems promote a greater sense of accountability because you are not solely accountable to yourself but accountable to the greater community. We should be as intentional about how we hold students accountable to the high standards that we set for them and those that they set for themselves as we are about what we teach students on an annual basis. The absence of rules and structure is predicated on the same deficit-based thinking about students that informs the control-based systems. One approach believes that students are deficient in their decision-making and thus must be controlled. The other approach believes that students are deficient in their ability to respond to reasonable consequences and make behavior changes. In this way it is not surprising we see schools swinging wildly from one side of the extreme to the other, with students getting whiplash in the process.

Anti-racist discipline structures seek to hold students to high expectations. They just give stakeholders like students and their parents power in defining what those high expectations are. Anti-racism isn't about removing or reducing the expectations that we have for students. It is about identifying and replacing racist expectations with anti-racist ones. Freedom teaching is about replacing discipline systems that value control with discipline systems that reward students for making productive choices and teach students who don't how to do that.

Reinforcing the Behaviors We Want

Teaching is about connecting with the heart, mind, and soul of a student, while our primary job is to share information and enhance student knowledge. There are several psychological prerequisites for our students to be in a place where they can maximize their learning. The last chapter talks about how radical hope really means to hope completely. Our hope and belief that we can change educational systems inside of our classrooms and schools has to be thorough. This is why aligning one's hope with action is so critically important. Among the greatest thieves of hope in schools or classrooms are the times when students struggle to grasp content, when they behave in undesirable ways, or when systems break down. It is one thing to be hopeful when it feels like things are going our way. It is another thing entirely when it feels like you just can't seem to get consistent traction with a group of students. Dr. Jeff Duncan-Andrade talks about how hope is one of the most significant tools that we have to support young people in navigating toxic stress situations and social trauma.[1] Hope is the vehicle that can transport students from being critically aware about their social situation to them believing that they have the agency to take action and change it.

The problem is that for our students who struggle both inside and outside of the classroom, many of them go to the least hopeful version of school. A student who is behind academically might be held out of PE, music, or art in order to get extra time in math or ELA. I am not suggesting that the desire to get a student extra time in a subject that they are struggling in is a negative thing. I am just suggesting that losing out on another content area, especially one that promotes movement or creativity, rarely has the desired effect that we are looking for. If a student feels invested in, or successful, in those settings, then they are losing a crucial part of their day that makes them feel good and hopeful at school. Instead of their additional time working on math or ELA feeling like a gift, it instead feels like a punishment. I have worked in schools where students who misbehave are punished by losing time talking to their peers at lunch or by losing their ability to play at recess. When I ask if these interventions are successful, I am frequently told yes. If I dig a bit further I learn that it is the same students over and over again who are receiving these punishments.

A common form of negative punishment in schools is leaving students behind from field trips if they don't meet some sort of predetermined criteria. Usually this is framed as positive reinforcement, suggesting that the trip is something to be earned. The real function of this tactic is the exclusion of misbehaving students. This dynamic in practice frequently becomes far more about not being left behind than about actually going on the field trip. The students who behave how adults want them to behave on a regular basis probably aren't really being incentivized or disincentivized by this practice. But the students who don't fit neatly into behavior expectations are the ones targeted by this intervention. In some cases, a single infraction can cause a student to "lose the trip." According to hope theory, "higher hope corresponds with superior academic and athletic performance, greater physical and psychological well-being, and enhanced interpersonal relationships."[2] Along with a plethora of benefits that research finds for centering hopefulness in our students and ourselves, this should tell us that our students who struggle the most need to be exposed to a hope-filled environment rather than removed from it.

If we are not thoughtful about our systems, then some students go to a version of school with limited access to play, social time, enrichment courses, and activities outside of school. It is not simply enough to have access to all of these opportunities—who is able to take advantage of them, and why? Do we disallow or discourage certain students from engaging in after-school activities because we are ready for them to go home at the end of the day? The students we struggle with the most famously have the best immune systems. The students whom you secretly wish would sprinkle in a sick day every now and then seem never to miss school. This means that these students are looking for something, especially as they get older and have alternative choices. The question is: Do we have the thing they are looking for?

So how do we teach and reinforce the behaviors that we want in ways that don't steal hope from our students? Let's begin with some definitions in order to assess where we are currently.

If the consequence adds something, it is a positive reinforcement/punishment. For example, giving students extra time to play outside after a week of hard work is positive reinforcement. You added more outside time to reinforce the behavior of hard work. Positive punishment, on the other hand, would be if you added more work time in lieu of outside time because students weren't completing their work to your satisfaction. Negative reinforcement is if you remove something undesirable for the student, like additional homework if their practice time in class was utilized effectively. Negative punishment is rooted in taking away something desirable, like recess, in order to

Table 7.1   Positive/negative reinforcement/punishment.

	Reinforcement	Punishment
Positive	Something is *added* to *increase* the likelihood of a behavior.	Something is *added* to *decrease* the likelihood of a behavior.
Negative	Something is *removed* to *increase* the likelihood of a behavior.	Something is *removed* to *decrease* the likelihood of a behavior.

decrease a target behavior. Most research suggests that reinforcing the behaviors that we desire is more effective than punishing students to disincentivize behaviors that we don't desire.

Think about which students in your class, or in student populations more broadly, are most frequently placed in environments informed by punishment rather than reinforcement. Punishment, which is aimed at decreasing the likelihood of an undesirable behavior, typically reinforces fear more than it does learning. Students might choose to refrain from a certain behavior because they fear the consequences, or because they fear the adult who might impose the consequence. Teachers who rely heavily upon positive/negative punishments as a response to student misbehavior likely aren't teaching those students why that behavior is undesirable in the first place. The very same student who chooses to refrain from a behavior that negatively impacts their learning in your classroom might lean into that behavior in another classroom with a teacher they do not fear. A lot of the rhetoric about being tough on students, no-nonsense—or worst of all, "broken windows" rhetoric in schools—is rooted in the desire to maintain a school where students fear their teachers or the consequences that teachers have the ability to dole out.

Reinforcement doesn't always feel right either. If we lean heavily into positive reinforcement, it feels like we are rewarding children for doing the things that they are supposed to do. As far as negative reinforcement goes, most teachers and school leaders get this mixed up with positive punishment so you see it used less frequently as a strategy in schools. There is something particularly attractive about the idea that students would just be intrinsically motivated to do the right things in school simply because they are the right things to do. Out of fear of incentivizing students out of their intrinsic motivation, we often withhold rewards (positive reinforcement) at times and in places when rewards are both reasonable and effective. The older I grow, the more I realize that I seldom engage in activities that I am not required to do unless there is some type of positive or negative reinforcement. We don't work simply because the work is noble; we also work because it provides us the means to take care of our family. We might be more likely to continue to work out and eat well once people start noticing and commenting on our physique. Additionally, after a while of working out, some of the pain and soreness we felt in the beginning is lessened, which incentivizes us to continue or even try heavier weights.

Everything from the clothes we wear to the social groups we spend time around to how we leverage our social media has a lot to do with the reinforcements we receive. Students are providing us with positive and negative reinforcement all the time. When we work hard to plan a lesson and students are learning, laughing, and engaged, that reinforces the behavior of being well planned. When students are engaged in lessons that are relevant and interesting, you might also notice that they remove distractions, even going as far as correcting one another, because they are invested in the lesson. This is an example of students providing us with negative reinforcement, whether intentional or not. The point is we cannot be the only ones receiving reinforcement throughout the day. So before you withhold that reward, praise, or affirmation from a student because "that is just what they are supposed to do," think about how many things we do in life solely because it is the right thing to do with no reward or compensation whatsoever. Really, take a moment to actively think about it. My list is admittedly pretty short.

In my third or fourth year of teaching, I served as the grade-level chair for eighth grade. In this role I set a vision for the grade level and served as a liaison between the students, their teachers, and the administration. I've never cared more about a made-up job with no extra pay. Two stories particularly stand out to me that illustrate the power of reinforcing the behaviors that we want over punishing the behaviors that we do not want. Both of these stories are anecdotes about teachers on my grade level coming to me in need of support for students. In both cases these were teachers with more experience than I had and were both teachers whom I respected.

Anecdote #1

There was a student on our grade level who had been at our school since fifth grade; we will call him Terrence. Terrence was a sweet and funny kid, truly a pleasure to be around if you took the time to get to know him. He also frequently acted out in order to gain the attention of his peers or to be removed from academically stressful situations. In his most notable performance, he once lit some small "black cat" firecrackers in the back of a first-year teacher's class-room. Older, more mature, and with his pyrotechnic past behind him, Terrence entered my classroom. I found him to be a pleasure to teach and the times when he was disruptive I recognized was usually the symptom of social anxiety. As he navigated the lower grades I perceived him to be popular amongst his peers and attrib-uted his hijinks to his desire to keep his "fans" entertained.

When I actually got the opportunity to teach him it was the opposite of that. Terrence struggled to make friends and students teased him about his height and weight. His grand gestures for attention rarely brought the attention that he desired from his peers or from his teachers. To my surprise, this kid with a big personality and reputation was actually pretty lonely, shy, and misunderstood. At this time the dean of students, Mr. Troy—who was a close friend of mine and the only other Black man working on the grade level— and I would either work out in my classroom or play basketball together after school. One day Terrence saw us working out and asked if he could join. I called up his mom and once she got over the initial shock that he was volunteering to exercise, she excitedly gave her permission and commitment to pick him up after the workouts.

I speak a lot in this book about avoiding deficit-based mindsets about kids and yet at this moment I found myself doubting Terrence's commitment. Terrence didn't play basketball with the other kids at recess; we were doing P90x at the time and the high-intensity work-outs were very challenging and not fun. I thought he might stick around for a few days and quit or that Mr. Troy and I would have to drag him through the workouts. Yet again I was fooled. Terrence worked extremely hard and was very focused during the workouts.

After a while he was the primary driver for why we were working out because neither of us wanted to quit or take a day off before he did. Terrence, Mr. Troy, and I began to form a closer relationship and used that time to discuss his hopes, dreams, goals, and aspirations inside and outside of school.

One day, Terrence's math teacher told me that he was struggling in her class. Apparently he had an outburst because he received an after-school punishment that would conflict with our regular workout time. Recognizing how invested the student was in working out after school, the teacher asked if I would leverage it as an incentive. If Terrence did all of his work in math class then he could work out with us. If he didn't complete his work or misbehaved, then he would lose the privilege of staying after and working out. In order to decrease the likelihood that Terrence misbehaved, the teacher was asking me to remove the incentive of working out. This is a clear example of negative punishment.

To be abundantly clear, I was disappointed to hear that Terrence was not behaving to the best of his ability in math. It was important to me that he got his act together, but not like this. We should aim to use consequences that reinforce the behaviors that we want whenever possible. If you make the choice that a punishment is the best course of action, then you also have to assess the negative side effects of said punishment. Besides being less effective, the issue with punishment is that punishment's power is staked on either the fear, frustration, or disappointment of the child. In this case the target behavior is for Terrence to decrease his disruptions in math. The punishment, however, sought to take something away that was physically and socially healthy for the student.

My assessment was that threatening his after-school workouts would not improve the target behavior. I actually believed that it would have the opposite effect. What I was sure that it would do is limit the student's access to a healthy outlet at school. After-school exercise was improving Terrence's mood, health, and enthusiasm for being in school, so threatening to take all of that away would be short-sighted. At this moment I had to prioritize the student and tell my colleague, whom I respected, that exercise time was not on the table and that we would have to brainstorm something else to get to the desired outcome. Educating the entire child means looking past the first option or the immediate option in order to find the best option. Working out after school with Terrence was a gateway to improve his behavior in school. Rather than dangling the workouts like a carrot, I instead used that time to deepen my relationship with Terrence such that we could talk through his problems in math and come up with solutions together.

Anecdote #2

In this story it is actually my students who provide the correction. I was cleaning up my classroom during my planning period and my classroom neighbor who taught ELA walked into my classroom and asked if she could speak with me. I noticed she was visibly upset and on the verge of tears. I asked her to take a seat and braced myself for the worst. I wondered what my students could have done to elicit this reaction and prepared myself emotionally for the rest of my planning period to be spent getting to the bottom of it.

At the time I was teaching about stereotypes in class. Students were learning about how historic stereotypes about Black people were crafted in order to justify oppressive policies and undermine Black progress. We discussed the "sambo," the "mammy," the "sapphire," and the "buck" stereotypes and students thought of modern examples of how these stereotypes are pushed in the media. This lesson was in a unit that I taught after the state test in which students examined the role of Black people in film from 1915 to the present day. We used all of the historical thinking skills and writing skills that we practiced throughout the year and applied them to this unit, which I adapted from a course I took in college to be appropriate for middle schoolers.

Once my friend who taught next door took a seat, she began to explain what happened in her class. This teacher was white, 99% of our students were Black, and an image that she showed in her PowerPoint offended some of the students. One of the reasons why I taught my students so thoroughly on the history of race and racism is so they could be equipped to defend themselves if ever faced with it directly. She went on to explain that she showed an edited image of Oprah that made her look angry or enraged. The image was meant to illustrate a literary point but it didn't sit well with the class. After class four students confronted her about her choice of imagery on the slide. While talking about this confrontation the teacher broke into tears. It was at this point that I realized for the first time that her tears were not tears of sadness, anger, or frustration but rather tears of pride. She explained to me that these eighth-grade students sat her down and calmly explained to her the definition of the "sapphire" stereotype of the "angry Black woman." They let her know that while her image choice was likely inadvertent, they wanted to see Black role models of theirs presented in an accurate light.

The teacher went on to explain that she felt educated and humanized by their response. She said that in that moment the roles were flipped and her students were able to address her as the intellectual authority on a topic. Because these students had the language to express their concerns and frustrations, they were able to engage with her from a place of empathy rather than a place of anger or dismissing her as a "racist." In the end the students gave her a valuable lesson, they shared hugs, and the teacher was able to adjust the slide for the rest of her lessons. She was in my room not to ask me to chastise the children, or to chastise me for what I was teaching them. Instead she was there to praise them and to thank me for helping to facilitate that type of interaction.

If my students chose positive punishment and scolded the teacher for her choices they would have been no less right, but it might have led their teacher to get defensive and the learning opportunity for both parties could have been missed. Instead they chose to center their critique on increasing the likelihood of seeing positive images of people that look like them in their lessons. They did this by demonstrating empathy and understanding for the teacher even though she was the one who was in error. The teacher additionally reinforced these students' use of their resistant capital by coming to her directly to express their concerns. It is not easy to correct an adult. It requires even more skill to correct an adult across racial differences about an issue with racism. This teacher modeled excellently the type of affirming response the students needed in that moment. You hear more and more that providing students of color with an affirming education on issues of race is divisive, or somehow anti-white. I love this story for several reasons, but mainly because it shows that when we give students the tools and the language to understand racism, we give them the power to address it in transformative ways.

Take a moment to think about times when you have utilized all four types of responses to student behavior. Was it more effective when you worked in earnest to increase a behavior (reinforcement), or was it more effective for you when you worked to decrease a behavior (punishment)? When choosing punishment, did you take the time to think about the unintended impact of your choices and did you weigh the costs and benefits?

Turning radical hope into practice means being intentional about the choices that we make inside and outside of the classroom. To ensure our hope for students is complete and thorough, we have to be aware of our own power and the power of the students that we serve. Whatever actions we take to increase the power of our students serves to decrease the predictable behavioral choices that students make when they feel powerless. Having the type of hope that allows us to have the audacity to believe that we can change longstanding systems means also understanding the small things we can do in our personal practice to validate that hope. I cannot reiterate enough that hoping big is hard, but it is the only thing that has ever preceded change. Every movement, every revolution, every social reform has started with people who have dared to hope radically.

Misbehaviors Are an Opportunity to Teach

Students are going to misbehave. It doesn't matter how strong the culture of your school or classroom is; students will find ways to push the boundaries of your expectations. I work with adults and they still find ways to push the boundaries of my expectations. Once we normalize that misbehavior, we inevitably have to strike a balance between holding students accountable for their actions and teaching students replacement behaviors. Teaching is difficult enough without the introduction of unnecessary distractions. When misbehaviors occur at inopportune times it can be so frustrating that we lose sight of the fact that consequences are teaching opportunities too.

Misbehaviors certainly can, and often do, disrupt the flow of a class, but that does not mean that they have to disrupt your ability to teach. Some of the most important lessons I learned in school came as a result of me making the wrong choices. Some of my most memorable teachers were the ones who saw through my behavior and found ways to humanize me while teaching me a valuable lesson. Punishing students over and over again is more likely to reinforce the undesirable behavior than it is to change it. What good is an umbrella if you are already soaked? Once you get into the habit of raining down demerits, strikes, and punishments on kids, it is natural for them at some point to stop caring. Remember, freedom teaching is about the deliberate actions that we can take to enhance the freedom of all children. Consequences can be liberatory too when they realign students to their needs and priorities.

This is why it is so important to set goals with students and to keep track of those goals. This is why it is important to identify the values that students hold dear and the values that are important to their families. Believe it or not, students crave structure and consistency. If you are currently picturing the kid who seemed determined to sow chaos in your classroom, yes, that student too. Because students learn best in environments where their expectations are clear, they are invested in those expectations and discipline is levied out consistently.

Structure doesn't mean that the students are compliance robots. Structure can look a lot of different ways. What it does mean is that the classroom systems are executed with fluency, and when there are breaches of the classroom rules, those breaches are clear to everyone in the classroom community. Clear, consistent, and affirming structure is liberating to students because it removes additional obstacles for learning. If you ask your students who their favorite teacher is, a vast majority of the time it isn't the teacher whose class they can get away with the most in. It is probably the teacher whose classroom they learn the most in and feel the most successful. Once we start with the baseline understanding that our students want to be successful in our classrooms, then we can create discipline systems that are in alignment with that central desire.

If we waver from the core belief that our students want to be successful and do well in our class, it is easy to slip into unproductive power struggles with kids. The goal of freedom teaching is to expand students' power over their education and to give them the tools to wield that power responsibly. More frequently than not, power struggles with students and overt displays of authority pull both the teacher and the student further away from their shared goals. Just like we can be sensitive when students misbehave, young people are often sensitive as well, and they are especially sensitive to being embarrassed in front of their peers. Displays of authority that embarrass children usually serve to push them into a fight-or-flight response. The student might shut down, and long-term damage can be done to your relationship with them and, as an extension of that, to their learning. Or the student might fight back, which usually leads to unnecessary escalation in order to save face in front of the rest of the students.

Sharing power with students and finding solutions to problems that hold students accountable for their actions while maintaining their integrity is usually the best option. As much as it can seem scary to intentionally cede some of your power to students, I learned pretty quickly during my time teaching that I would rather deal with a student who was operating from a place of empowerment rather than a place of powerlessness. As discussed in Chapter 4, people who feel powerless are more likely to engage in destructive behavior than constructive behavior. The goal of freedom teaching is to develop cognitively, socially, emotionally empowered students. Exposing students to discipline practices that teach and humanize is a critical step in this process. Remember, radical change means change that is thorough and complete. Too many schools are engaged in "Zoom attire" anti-racism. They have the right faces on the walls, and teachers are using the right language. From the waist up things look pretty good. However, if you look under the desk, the discipline systems are still exclusionary. Teachers are still hoarding power over students, or even worse, students aren't being held accountable for their actions at all. Underneath the desk the school is still wearing the same sweatpants from the night before.

Here are some things to consider when using discipline as a means to teach rather than punish.

Identify Traits and Skills of Empowered Students

Our students' behavior is most frequently a reflection of our practice. With that in mind, we have to have an idea of what it is that we desire to see from our students. Discipline that solely places a spotlight on undesirable behavior quickly devolves into policing. What is it that we see in our students that we want to continue to draw out, reaffirm, and highlight? What does an empowered student look like and what teacher behaviors allow our students to best show off their light?

Please do not mistake this for "character education." It is actually quite the opposite. The push for "character education," especially for children in urban schools, centered on the deficit-based theory that these students lack certain character traits. It also assumes that "fixing" a student's character will solve the problem. But the problems weren't created by the students; the problems were created by the injustice these students face. "Character education" is an individualized solution to a systemic problem. We are not assuming that our students are in need of us to "teach" them how to have good character. We are instead making the assertion that we will know that we are creating the optimal conditions for students to learn when we put students in the position to be their best selves. Consequences should realign students to their potential and remind them of the standard that they are capable of upholding. By identifying traits of empowered students, we can use that as our baseline when assessing how we hold students accountable. It gives us an internal sounding board to ask ourselves if we are humanizing our students or dehumanizing them.

Identify the traits your students exhibit when they feel empowered.

Traits and Skills of Empowered Students

- They are adaptable.
- They are assertive.
- They are autonomous.
- They are engaged.
- They are open-minded.
- They are optimistic.
- They are resilient.
- They are respectful.
- They are self-aware.
- They are self-confident.
- They have high self-esteem.
- They problem-solve.
- They take initiative.

Consider the Effect of Consequences

Consequences that humiliate can damage a student's self-esteem, optimism, and self-confidence. Before administering that consequence, you should ask yourself what the larger impact might be on the child. Challenging a student who rushed through an assignment with more rigorous work might remind a student of their resilience and ability to problem-solve. Depending on the situation, this might be an appropriate consequence. Pushing a student to reflect on their tone with their peer might give a student an opportunity to flex their self-awareness and respect for others. Punishing a student by removing them from class undermines their ability to solve problems, to adapt, and to be engaged. If we want to create an environment where our students get to lean into and build upon their best attributes, we have to identify those best attributes and be mindful when our actions infringe upon students' ability to be their best. Consequences should remind students who they are when they are at their best, and realign them to that version of themselves.

Align Consequences to Student Goals and Values

Set time-based goals with students. Some of these goals should be short-term easy wins. Some of these goals should be year-long goals. Some of the goals should be life-long goals. Help students define their "why," so when school feels tedious or abstract you can remind students that they are working toward something. Besides themselves, who do they work hard for? Who else do they hope to benefit by accomplishing their educational and professional goals? Help your students identify that person or those people.

If you have ever gone for a run or to the gym with someone else, or made a group commitment or pledge to make some lifestyle change, you likely know it can be easier at times to quit on yourself rather than on someone else. Ask your students about their values. It is okay to have generic classroom rules and expectations, but it is even more powerful if those expectations are sourced from your students. Have your students put these reminders somewhere they can see them. Laminate them and tape them to their binder. Attach a sleeve to their desk and task a student with passing them out at the beginning of class and collecting them at the end of class. Make space on a bulletin board and display them all there.

When you have a strong relationship with your students, most undesirable behaviors are small, quick, and minorly disruptive. For those behaviors that need to be addressed but don't require a significant intervention, have students connect their choices to their values and/or goals. "Are these choices getting you closer or further away from your goals?" "Are these behaviors in alignment with your why?" "What do you need from me to help you realign your behavior with your values?" Set up peer accountability partners and teach them how to facilitate check-ins. Incentivize students to hold each other accountable in affirming ways by providing positive reinforcement for students who uplift the classroom community. Invest your students in each other and in the idea that individual choices also impact the group.

In effect, you are holding students accountable to their own expectations of themselves rather than to your expectations. You are trying to actively teach your students that their actions matter. If students are consistently struggling to uphold their own values, it is likely an indication that they are struggling with something or there is an unmet need that needs to be addressed. How students respond to their expectations of themselves is important data that can help us understand the appropriate way to respond. This strategy is about constantly reaffirming students in their why, their expectations of themselves, and their values. We are trying to help students build their ability to align their actions with their values and to reflect when the two are misaligned.

Aim for Consequences That Are Restorative, Student-Driven, and Community-Focused

Students should feel accountable to each other and they should feel like they are in the driver seat for creating the ideal conditions for learning. Restorative approaches focus on repairing the harm done over punishing the harm doer. Restorative approaches offer both a proactive and a reactive set of tools for educators. Community circles are proactive interventions aimed at strengthening relationships and building community and empathy among students. Facilitated dialogues offer students the ability to build skills in how to navigate conflict, in de-escalation techniques, and in how to peer mediate. Problem-solving circles and restorative conferences address conflict, clear up misunderstandings, and create mutually agreed conditions for moving forward.

The strength of restorative approaches is that they are student centered. They seek to address causes rather than symptoms and they aim to provide long-term solutions to problems. The challenge of restorative approaches is that they require training to execute. The process takes more time and it requires buy-in from all involved parties. I have seen schools shift to a restorative approach without the aforementioned considerations and have found themselves in a middle ground between punitive systems and restorative. If you are going to do restorative approaches in your school or classroom you truly have to commit, or else you likely will not see the results that you are looking for.

As much as possible, discipline systems should be student driven. Create peer-mediation groups. Create opportunities for peer-to-peer mentorship, or an alumni mentorship program. Invest students in the idea that our actions are interconnected and implore students to be keepers of the communal norms.

At this point some of you are rolling your eyes as if I asked you to open a snack bag and eat just one chip. "If I had the ability to do that I wouldn't be reading this book!" The reason it seems so implausible to some people that students would be bearers of a school's or a classroom's culture is because the systems those students are existing in are strictly punitive. Asking students to uphold a culture that disempowers students is effectively asking them to police their peers. I don't blame students for being disinvested in the thought of upholding those cultural norms, because they are not cultural norms at all.

Asking students to uphold culture norms that empower themselves and their peers is asking them to participate in authoring their collective liberation. This is why the "all-in" approach is so critical. If your school or classroom is not clear on what it wants to be, students won't be clear either. You cannot expect students to willfully uphold norms that they don't feel invested in. If students don't feel invested in the community norms, that should cause us to question if our priorities are in the right place.

Our school norms should extend to the community that our school serves. We should know who our students' "person," or "people" are because almost every kid has one, and if they don't it is even more urgent that we identify someone who can fulfill that role for them. A student's "person" is who they can talk to when they are in crisis, the person they want to make proud, or the person they don't want to disappoint. It might be a person they look up to, or a person who holds the keys to an activity that they value. Either way it is a person of significance in the student's life.

For some students their person might be a cafeteria worker, the nurse, a custodian, or somebody in the office. For others it might be a coach or a religious leader in their community. For others it is a mother or father, an aunt or uncle, a "big cousin," a sibling or grandparent. It takes a village to raise a child. When schools are not connected to their students' "village," we lose out on a powerful and essential resource. In many circumstances schools find a student's "person" after the student has breached a norm or expectation. This is like going to the bank and trying to withdraw funds without making a deposit. Then when we're facing "insufficient funds," far too many of us are ready to write off the student's extended community. These are relationships that need to be formed based on the mutual love and understanding of the potential of the student. These relationships should be nurtured like all other relationships. Whenever possible they should be centered around joy, celebration of accomplishments, and pushing students to break past their personal barriers. Then when we need their person to show up to help us hold a student accountable after an incident of bad judgment, they will be there.

Aim for Consequences That Are Consistent, Predictable, and Compassionate

It is rarely effective when educators make decisions based on fear. Choosing to ignore student misbehavior and breaches of school culture is a fear-based response and as a result cannot be anti-racist. There seems to be a trend in which schools are recognizing the errors of their ways and are working to dismantle racist discipline practices. This is a good thing. The problem is that far too many of these schools aren't replacing racist discipline systems with anti-racist ones. The result is the absence of discipline and account-ability, which ultimately comes from the same deficit-based think-ing as the racist systems that preceded them.

The pendulum swings from strict, restrictive, and exclusionary discipline, based on the belief that students would misbehave if given a dose of freedom, to unclear, inconsistent, and in some cases nonexistent discipline, based on the belief that students can't be held to a high behavioral standard without treating them like they are prisoners. Both of these approaches lead to unfavorable out-comes for children, and the second approach usually drives schools to an even more punitive version of the first approach—after lamenting the failure of discipline reform.

Schools should have rules, the rules should be enforced, and the expectations should be consistent and predictable. School rules should be culturally affirming, they should center students, and they should center purpose over power. Students should know what is expected of them because they should also expect it of themselves and their peers. Students should be aware of the fact that the adults in the building care enough about them to hold them accountable to being the best version of themselves they can be in the moment. This of course leaves room for students to make mistakes and to learn from them. This of course means accounting for the realities that students face at home and how those realities impact the ver-sion of them that we get in school.

When you care about someone, you tell them the things they want to hear and the things they need to hear. This should be no different than our relationship with our students. We hold them to high standards because we know that they can achieve them. The problem is that far too many schools mistake Eurocentric standards for high standards. When we involve students and their families in the making and maintenance of school culture, we can assure that we are all working toward the same goals.

Notes

1. Jeff Duncan Andrade, "Note to Educators: Hope Required When Growing Roses in Concrete," Askwith Forum, Annual Alumni of Color Conference, February 26, 2010, Harvard Graduate School of Education, YouTube video, 2:02:36, posted April 28, 2021, https://www.youtube.com/watch?v=8z1gwmkgFss&ab_channel=HarvardGraduateSchoolofEducation.

2. Kevin L. Rand and Jennifer S. Cheavens, "Hope Theory," in *The Oxford Handbook of Positive Psychology*, ed. C. R. Snyder, Shane J. Lopez, Lisa M. Edwards, and Susana C. Marques (Oxford: Oxford University Press, 2012), 323–33.

Chapter 8
Cultivating a Classroom That Values Cultural Wealth

It isn't anything revolutionary to suggest that schools should be spaces that affirm the students inhabiting them. Schooling should inspire creativity in students and a natural desire to acquire knowledge. It is difficult to feel invested in an environment that doesn't encourage or support you, and almost impossible in environments that are hostile. It is clear that we need to create and sustain environments in which students feel encouraged and valued. Students feeling valued in their school environments are far too often treated like a side dish rather than the main course. Affirmation is central to student socioemotional development as well as student academic progress. This chapter is going to dive into the benefits of intentional cultural affirmation in schools. It really isn't a complex concept: students learn better when they see themselves reflected in their curriculum.

So why is it that when we talk about creating classrooms where students' culture and identity are affirmed, we are frequently met with limiting beliefs?

- "I can't affirm the culture and identity of students if I do not belong to their cultural group."
- "I teach a diverse group of students. I surely can't affirm all of their cultures"
- "Focusing on culture and identity is a departure from the state standards and I already have limited time to teach my students to pass the state test."
- "Teaching culturally affirming content is great, but does it set students up for success in college and other academic environments?"

If we are to teach in ways that promote liberation for all students, one of the things we have to challenge is to question the things we do that we assume to be "neutral" or "impartial." As Howard Zinn reminds us, "You can't be neutral on a moving train."[1] I personally believe that every school in the United States, or at the very least the ones that I have interacted with, teaches cultural competence. Teaching a culturally competent and culturally affirming curriculum isn't really the issue. I have seen schools across the entire country do this exceptionally well. It is just that these schools are teaching cultural competence and understanding of the dominant cultures in the United States. In my education I was instructed to master dominant patterns of speech, the greetings and the salutations of the dominant culture, and patterns of humor, not to mention that the baseline narrative that undergirded a vast majority of my education was written about and from dominant perspectives.

Most schools are proficient at centering white, patriarchal, heteronormative, middle- and upper-middle-class values and narratives. It is common in our practice to think of certain policies and practices in schools as "neutral" and then think of culturally relevant and affirming practices as a deviation from that neutrality. This mindset positions us to believe that engaging in culturally affirming practices is something extra that we are doing for the edification of our students of color. We would better serve our students if we actually analyzed the roots of the practices, procedures, expectations, norms, and our curriculum to ensure there is balance. If we did this, we would likely find that there is a significant imbalance between the things that validate the dominant culture in schools and things that validate students who exist outside of dominant cultures. When framed this way, we see that there is a dire need to provide students from marginalized backgrounds with spaces that affirm their culture and identity as well.

Note that I said "as well," because this isn't about not affirming white students, or male students, or heterosexual students, or any other group. It is about the fact that we are likely already doing those things, so we have to focus on making sure that students who exist outside of those identity groupings are affirmed by school too.

Culturally Affirming Education

Anyone who has spent any amount of time with natural Black hair likely knows that your hair depends upon you finding the right things to put in it. When traveling, my mom would always pack her own shampoo and conditioner. As a kid I would think, "but the hotel usually provides that stuff." I realize now that the reason why many Black people with natural hair don't use the hotel samples is because while they clean your hair, they also strip Black hair of the natural oils that protect our hair from being damaged.

Providing students of color with a "color-blind" education is a lot like asking Black people to use hair-care products that aren't good for our hair. You will get an education, but you might be stripped of your cultural worth and value in the process. Our education system provides the illusion that it serves all students, but it ultimately damages some of them. Even worse, those students can easily conclude that there is something wrong with *them*, rather than with the fact that the product we provide for them isn't a good match. I learned so many valuable lessons in school. I learned about great philosophers, artists, writers, historical figures, inventors, and innovators. I can count on my hands how many of them looked like me or came from a similar background that I did.

We accept that different cars might need different fuel. We know that different people have different dietary requirements. My brother and I grew up in the same household with the same parents, and our parents knew that we needed different things for us to reach our full potential inside and outside of school. So it shouldn't be revolutionary to acknowledge that a "one-size-fits-all," "color-blind" education is not only *not* neutral—it's detrimental for many students. This is why we reiterate that anti-racism in education is not simply a moral obligation. We engage in anti-racist practices because they are the structurally right thing to do. Students learn best when they are in school environments that take into consideration their unique needs. Creating classrooms that are culturally competent ensures that our systems meet students where they are, rather than our students having to contort themselves in order to fit into our systems. We need to address the impact of social and environmental factors so that all students can receive an education *and* retain their cultural worth and value. And yes, noticing the impact of social and environmental factors certainly makes our job more difficult, but freedom teaching requires it.

What Is Cultural Wealth?

Tara J. Yosso's exceptional paper "Whose Culture Has Capital?" defines cultural wealth as "an array of knowledge, skills, abilities and contacts possessed and utilized by Communities of Color to survive and resist macro and micro-forms of oppression."[2] Cultural wealth is the sum of the knowledge and skills that people from marginalized communities acquire and pass down by virtue of navigating oppressive systems. Think of cultural wealth as a grab bag of survival skills that have been carefully curated and maintained over time. The beautiful thing about cultural wealth is that you do not have to teach students how to have it. Students already come to school equipped with this valuable resource. A student's process of developing their cultural wealth is frequently unconscious as a result of the reality that these funds of knowledge are not elevated and valued by society. It is about us as the adults in the building creating environments that value our student's cultural wealth. Overcoming Racism's director of impact, Ahmed, compares cultural wealth to the varying types of currency one might carry if they are traveling internationally. You can have all of the wealth in the world but if your currency is not accepted somewhere then it is essentially worthless. Schools shouldn't be a place where students' wealth is only valued when it is validated by the dominant gaze.

Deficit-based perspectives focus on "fixing" the groups of students that belong to ethnic minorities. These theories and the policies that accompany them blame trends of underachievement among groups of students of color on the students themselves. Cultural wealth theory is something different entirely; instead of positioning students as deficient this concept positions all students as inherently valuable.

Tara J. Yosso outlines six different forms of cultural wealth, which are explained in the following sections.

Aspirational Capital

Aspirational capital is "the ability to maintain hopes and dreams for the future, even in the face of real and perceived barriers."[3] Students and families show aspirational capital in an abundance of ways. School is a long-term commitment. A student has to believe that coming to school every day and working hard for over a decade of their life will yield them the quality of life that they desire in the future. For some families that has been true, but for many families schooling hasn't had a one-to-one correlation with long-term success.

The vast majority of students I taught were aspiring first-generation college students. These students nonetheless truly believed in their ability to go to college and to leverage that for their long-term success. I think we take for granted how special that is. A vast majority of the students I served lived under the poverty line. For many of them just coming to school every day required aspirational capital. We have to celebrate the vastness of our students' dreams while providing them with a clear roadmap on how to actualize them.

Here are some ways you can elevate your students' aspirational capital in your schools and classrooms:

- Set goals with students and track their progress from year to year.
- Empower students to lead conferences.
- Create student leadership councils.
- Understand your students' home values.
- Keep students updated on the score of the game.
- Provide students with internship opportunities.
- Engage students with experiential learning on field trips.
- Utilize role-play projects in the classroom.
- Incorporate goal-setting prompts into student assignments.
- Set up rotating accountability partnerships between students in class.
- Expose students to mentorship programs.

Linguistic Capital

Linguistic capital is "the intellectual and social skills attained through communication experiences in more than one language and/or style." Yosso's text outlines the vast utility of linguistic capital, from the power of the oral tradition in communities of color to how these communities develop the ability to communicate in multiple languages and dialects. Yosso articulates that students bring to school with them "skills [that] may include memorization, attention to detail, dramatic pauses, comedic timing, facial affect, vocal tone, volume, rhythm, and rhyme."[4] These skills can and should be leveraged to support learning and they should be celebrated in the classroom.

For years schools have used deficit-based framing to describe emerging bilingual students, almost as if to say that students who are not native-born English speakers are somehow deficient. In reality the skills that these students are developing to be able to speak multiple languages is a huge asset. In most countries around the world, all students are emerging bilingual students. I think about my own experience with learning how to code-switch in my home. Growing up, my mother was very strict about my grammar. If my brother or I used African American Vernacular English

(AAVE), slang or the like in the house, it was swiftly corrected. She would tell us something to the extent of "That is incorrect. The correct way to say that is _____."

"Code-switching" is a vital tool that people of color leverage in professional and academic spaces. I am glad that my mother prioritized my ability to understand and speak the dominant language fluently. With that being said, as I have grown older I have come to realize the power in my ability to switch between dialects with ease. Black people have developed AAVE over centuries and have wielded it as a tool of inspiration, creativity, and even survival. There was nothing "wrong" or incorrect about my home language. In fact it offered me a competitive advantage and an ability to navigate diverse spaces. I realize now that I didn't have to learn to code-switch for my own edification. I had to learn to code-switch because when I went into a college, a job interview, a bank, or some other formal environment, I had to switch dialects because the person I was engaging with most likely could not. If I had grown up with that framing, I would not have grown up believing that speaking my home language was something to be ashamed of or something that was deserving of scorn.

From students who translate for their parents, to students who have notebooks full of rap lyrics and poetry, to students who speak a different language with their grandparents overseas, linguistic capital is a powerful intellectual tool.

Here are some ways you can elevate your students' linguistic capital in your schools and classrooms:

- Affirm the home languages of your students.
- Engage students in multiple modalities of learning and assessment.
- Think about what participation can look like for a diverse set of students—using whiteboards, writing at their desks, engaging in seminars, and so on.
- Host heritage celebrations for students, families, and the community.
- Make connections with the funds of knowledge that students bring into the classroom.

- Provide opportunities for parents to provide cultural programming in students' native languages and dialects.
- Translate materials into multiple languages.
- Create alternate assessment opportunities.
- Provide students with access to foreign language courses—normalize bilingual programs.
- Incorporate forms of cultural expression into lessons (music, rhythm, rhyme, call and response, etc.).

Familial Capital

Familial capital is "cultural knowledge nurtured among family that carries a sense of community history, memory and cultural intuition."[5] For communities of color and for marginalized communities more broadly, it is not uncommon for people to form familial bonds outside of the traditional structure of the "nuclear family." In workshops I often ask participants who grew up with "play cousins." Almost immediately many of my participants of color raised their hands. Different cultures call these different things, but basically "play cousins" are the people you grow up with who you might not realize are not actually related to you until you are well into adulthood. Because people of color and ethnic minorities generally grow up in more communal cultures, it is not uncommon for us to form familial bonds with people to whom we are not actually related. A person might grow up with "aunties and uncles" who are really just their parents' close friends. A person might call the old lady down the street "abuela" even though she is technically just a woman who lives in the community. It is common in the Black tradition to call other Black people "brother" or "sister" even if you have never met.

Familial capital is a powerful tool because if students are already growing up in environments where family doesn't just mean the people who live under the roof with you, or people whose blood you share, then these same types of relationships can extend to the school environment. At the school where I worked in New Orleans, nobody embodied familial capital more than the custodians.

Mrs. Barbara, Mr. Charles, and Ms. Gabby were so critical to the operation of the school. They filled in the gaps that many of the teachers couldn't. They did students' hair so that they wouldn't be bullied, and fed students when they were hungry. They provided parental love, care, and guidance to students who were sad, angry, or frustrated in school and also had some of the best relationships with parents and grandparents. Whether a student needed a hug, a firm talking to, "the look," or some sage advice, the custodial team were familial capital superheroes. They also tended to have the best pulse on the latest tea (gossip) amongst the students. If two students were having a conflict I could usually count on Ms. Gabby to give me all of the details on what "had gone down." When we moved into a new school building, network leadership decided to hire a national custodial firm to manage the maintenance of the building. Ms. Barbara (who had been there since the school's founding), Mr. Charles, and Ms. Gabby were all relieved of their duties. The school suffered significantly from that decision.

Hiring the new custodial team saved the school money. If one was not to notice and value the familial capital that these individuals provided, then that might have seemed like a sound decision. However, it was anything but that; surely the school was saving money because these individuals were doing far more than what was within the scope of their job. If my network could have seen, valued, and compensated the invisible labor that those individuals were providing, the entire school community would have been better for it.

Here are some ways you can elevate your student's familial capital in your schools and classrooms:

- Create meaningful partnerships with the broader community.
- Host celebrations and assemblies for families.
- Document student connections in school records (siblings, cousins, etc.).
- Host parent town halls.
- Host bring-a-family-member-to-school days.
- Provide students with the opportunities to work in groups.

- Host weekly and, as needed, community circles to help students build deeper relationships with one another.
- Provide or connect families with community resources (mental health, technology literacy, financial literacy, etc.).
- Emphasize sports and other after-school activities.
- Refer to families instead of parents in communication.
- Host family onboarding at the beginning of the year.
- Preview learning targets, key projects, dates, and the like with families at the beginning of the year.
- Create a communication tree for families to share important information.
- Create a community library.

Social Capital and Navigational Capital

Social capital is "networks of people and community resources." Navigational capital is "skills of maneuvering through social institutions. Historically this refers to the ability to maneuver through institutions not created with Communities of Color in mind."[6] Let's think of social and navigational capital as a pair, or at the very least branches from the same tree.

Social and navigational capital serve different purposes but I like to think that the interventions that we use to elevate these forms of capital have significant overlap. Leveraging students' social capital is perhaps one of the most effective ways to unlock the potential of our student's navigational capital. Social capital leverages students' networks and their communities, as well as members of shared identity groups. Yosso's work talks about how people of color have leveraged their social capital as a source of "mutual aid" in these communities. Navigational capital comes into play as people in communities of color are forced to skillfully navigate institutions that were not created with them in mind.[7] Most people don't know that the Montgomery Improvement Association (social capital) created an intricate carpooling system to help boycotters get around during the Montgomery Bus Boycott (navigational capital).

In the United States, immigrant populations are more likely to live in multigenerational households (social capital), and participate in group economics (navigational capital). Historically Black, Asian, or Latinx fraternities and sororities and the existence of HBCUs or affinity spaces on historically white campuses are all examples of the overlap between leveraging social and navigational capital. Our students have to understand the power that comes with community. Of course, we want to develop students who can problem-solve and who have the ability to be self-sufficient. With that being said, drilling students who come from communal cultures with tired and outdated messages promoting rugged individualism is more often a recipe for failure than it is one for success. Togetherness is not only more likely to get our students further, it also is more likely to help to uplift the communities they come from.

In my classroom the Zulu word *ubuntu* was the core of our classroom rules. It was challenging to teach this word to students because there isn't a direct translation to a word in English. The closest I could probably get is the word "empathy," which is the "the ability to understand and share the feelings of another person." However *ubuntu* isn't simply about understanding or sharing another person's feelings. *Ubuntu* means "I am because we are." Some translations use up to eight or nine English words to describe *ubuntu*, words like "humaneness, justice, morality, solidarity, dignity, respect." *Ubuntu* describes the interconnectedness of the human experience.

Trying to live up to this word meant that we had to develop an understanding that our behaviors, choices, and actions didn't impact just us as individuals but the classroom as a whole. When I wasn't at my best, the classroom either struggled or my students helped to pick up the areas in which I was slacking. When students made choices that maximized their learning I tried to make sure to connect those choices to how they elevated our team. When students made choices that detracted from learning, those choices didn't impact only them but also the culture we were working to build collectively.

I wanted my students to build lifelong friendships with their peers but I also wanted them to understand that it was bigger than that. I needed my students to understand that the students who sat at the desks next to them were the seeds of a potential network. So when students shared their life's hopes and dreams, I connected them with the dreams of other students in the classroom. "If Davonte wants to own a sneaker shop, and you like sneakers, don't you want Davonte to be successful in his dream?" "If Elliany wants to be a dentist, wouldn't you trust her to take care of your teeth before you trust a stranger?" I asked my students how many of them had personal connections with engineers, lawyers, entrepreneurs, professional athletes, and so on. Some did, and most didn't. So then I asked them after we looked at the dreams that everyone wrote out in the classroom. "How many of you would have a personal connection to people in those professions if everyone in this classroom was able to accomplish their dreams?" Their hands flew toward the ceiling in unison.

Young people receive so many messages both inside and outside of school that push them to carry their burdens in isolation. We should teach our young people that their freedoms are intertwined. We must make implicit connections between their actions and the success of the group as a whole. We leverage our students' social and navigational capital by helping them to function as a team.

Here are some ways you can elevate your students' social and navigational capital in your schools and classrooms:

- Set goals with students and track them.
- Build intentional relationships with students.
- Create student social clubs and affinity clubs (e.g., "Houses" like in *Harry Potter*).
- Provide students with interest clubs, community service opportunities, and after-school programs.
- Create an alumni mentorship program.
- Create an accessible alumni network and database.
- Include students and families in the facilitation of family onboarding

- Establish parent and family connection programs for outside of school.
- Increase community partnerships.
- Host a speaker series.
- Host a career series to highlight different career paths throughout the year, rather than simply on a career day.
- Create and provide training for peer-to-peer tutoring and mentoring programs.
- Create and provide training for peer-to-peer conflict mediation groups.
- When appropriate, offer constructivist teaching and learning opportunities.
- Teach financial literacy courses. Engage your school community to see if there are parents or community members who would like to help teach students or their peers.
- Provide anti-racism training for parents, staff, and board members.
- Create a community-sourced shared resources repository.

Resistant Capital

Resistant capital is "knowledge and skills fostered through oppositional behavior that challenges inequality."[8] If you say the word "oppositional" in front of the word "behavior," educators break out in a cold sweat. But the reality is that oppositional behavior isn't our enemy. Our enemy is self-defeating oppositional behavior, when students oppose stated rules and expectations in a way that is self-defeating to that student's long-term goals. Misbehavior is most frequently the symptom of an unmet need. So if a student has a need that is going unmet, they might communicate that to the adult in the room in different ways. Sometimes that communication might come in the form of oppositional behavior.

We don't want to create a culture where we teach students to blindly comply with authority even when they feel like stated norms or expectations are unfair. The reality for people in marginalized communities is that unfortunately that liberty has not been afforded to us. Schools that serve children of color need to raise up the next generation of freedom fighters just like we cultivate future lawyers, doctors, barbers, entrepreneurs, teachers, and so on. So we must be clear that it is our job to teach students how to question authority in productive and transformative ways. Some of the best moments I have had in the classroom have come when I embraced students' ability to ask me clarifying questions, give me critical feedback, or suggest other ways to accomplish a stated task. If students are engaging in self-defeating forms of resistance—like refusing to complete academic tasks, being disruptive to their peers, or engaging in unsafe behavior—then this is a teaching opportunity.

We have to teach those students to identify what needs aren't being met for them and in those moments how to replace self-defeating behaviors with transformative behaviors. This is not always an easy thing to do; even adults struggle with self-regulation. When I am frustrated or upset I often become the least reliable version of myself when it comes to finding productive solutions. However, it didn't take me long to realize that if I was going to be a productive member of society, let alone teacher, I would have to find replacement behaviors for whatever my baseline instinct was when I am not in the best mood. Giving students the tools to regulate their emotions early and to search for productive solutions in moments when they feel like their needs are being unmet or they are being treated unfairly is critical. When we create a culture where students feel as if they do not have agency to question authority in helpful and productive ways, they are far more likely to lean into the self-defeating behaviors we are seeking to eliminate.

Here are some ways you can elevate your students' resistant capital in your schools and classrooms:

- Teach curriculum that actively builds student voice and agency.
- Create consistent and intentional feedback loops. (Do students have a way to provide feedback to adults in your building?)
- Offer mental health services that students and families can access.
- Empower students to engage in activism.

- Provide structures for direct family input in their students' education.
- Recognize and support resistance when it is transformative.
- Acknowledge the validity of student or family concerns.
- Teach about systemic oppression and ways that groups of people have worked together to subvert it.
- Give students space for self-advocacy.
- Bring in speakers from the community.
- Give students agency in important choices about the school and their education.
- Create a student government organization that has real authority and responsibilities.
- Host student and family feedback town halls.
- Provide students with surveys that are designed to better understand the student experience.
- Place a suggestion box in your classroom and make time to go over the suggestions with students.
- Promote restorative-discipline systems that are proactive as well as reactive.
- Implement de-escalation strategies like meditation and mindfulness in the classroom.

Take a moment to brainstorm ways that your school or your classroom already affirms these forms of cultural wealth. You can list these in Table 8.1.

Now take a moment to think about ways that your school or classroom could affirm this form of cultural wealth but isn't currently, and write these in Table 8.2 (you can download blank templates from www.overcomeracism.com/freedomteaching).

Standpoint Theory and Cultural Wealth

Standpoint theory is another helpful framework via which we can contextualize cultural wealth. According to Dr. Brenda J. Allen, "Standpoint theory strives to explain relationships between power

Table 8.1 Ways your practices elevate Tara Yosso's six different forms of cultural wealth.

Aspirational Capital	*Example: Providing students with rigorous content and the scaffolding that ensures their success*
Linguistic Capital	*Example: Asset-based emerging bilingual programming*
Familial Capital	*Example: Alumni mentorship program*
Social Capital	*Example: After-school interest-based electives*
Navigational Capital	*Example: Providing anti-racism training for teachers and staff*
Resistant Capital	*Example: Student advocacy groups*

Table 8.2   Ways your practices *could* elevate each form of cultural wealth.

Aspirational Capital

Linguistic Capital

Familial Capital

Social Capital

Navigational Capital

Resistant Capital

and the construction of knowledge." Standpoint theory asserts that our identities shape how we see and experience the world. As Allen explains, "Because society tends to recognize and value dominant ways of knowing, mainstream constructions of knowledge about social relations neglect to consider the viewpoints of subordinate groups. However, standpoint theory maintains that members of those marginalized groups have valuable insights."[9] Effectively, people who are pushed to the margins of society see the most holistic picture of the world.

Figure 8.1 illustrates the basic concept of the standpoint theory. People born into dominant identities are socialized in a society that centers their perspectives. This socialization can lead to a skewed vision of the world in which they exist. As a result of race, class, gender-based privilege, and so on, individuals socialized in dominant identities are likely insulated from several experiences and realities. In the United States, 80% of public school teachers are white. If you are white and educated in the public school system, chances are you're being educated by people who look like you. According to the Association of American Medical Colleges, 64% of US physicians identify as white,[10] so if you are white it's likely that your healthcare provider looks like you. A white child likely has access to children's books and cartoon characters that look like them. When that child goes to school they will likely learn of the intellectual contributions of people who look like them. When they turn on the TV they will see TV stars and movie stars who look like them and tell stories about people who look like them. If a white person feels unsafe, they might choose to call the police—and might not understand why a person from a different culture might not feel safe doing the same.

Our understanding of the world around us has a lot to do with how we are socialized to understand our lived reality in relation to others. If you are socialized in the dominant culture, seeking to understand the lived reality of people in marginalized cultures is a choice you can make—or not. The privilege of ignorance is paid for by the adverse experiences of people who are targeted by systems of oppression.

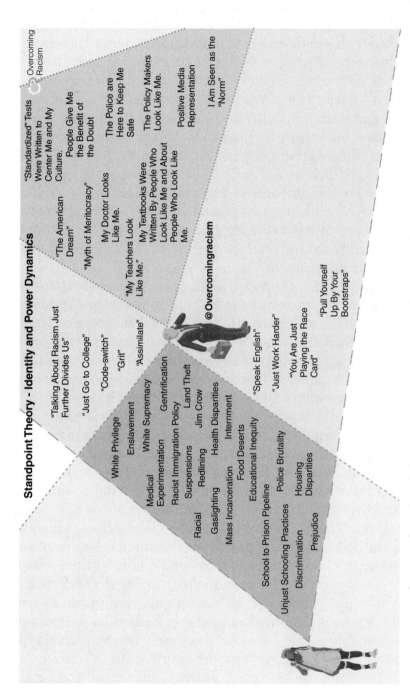

Figure 8.1   Visualization of standpoint theory.
Infographic by Overcoming Racism LLC.

Since there is no standard or universal curriculum about racism in this country, it goes untaught in most school systems. This means a white person can navigate the entire US education system, even into advanced degrees, and never develop an academic consciousness about what racism is and how it functions. Consequentially, entire worlds exist outside the vantage point of people with privilege. Furthermore, there are intentional efforts in this country to maintain dominant groups' "right" to ignorance. Dr. Beverly Daniel Tatum explains this in her essay "The Complexity of Identity," where she references the work of scholar Jean Baker Miller: "Miller points out that dominant groups generally do not like to be reminded of the existence of inequality. Because rationalizations have been created to justify the social arrangements, it is easy to believe that everything is as it should be."[11]

The calls to ban books and to outlaw teaching about racism in schools are an overt attempt to keep the vision of people in dominant groups obscured. This urge to protect the dominant gaze leads to dynamics like defensiveness and cognitive dissonance when people are confronted with the existence of their privilege. We see this dynamic play out publicly whenever marginalized groups dare to speak out for their rights. This is why chants of "Black Lives Matter" are drowned out by chants of "All lives matter." This is why all of our forms of protest throughout history, from sitting in to marching to silently kneeling, have faced great resistance and ire.

On the other side of this, people who exist in marginalized communities are forced to understand not only the realities of their own lived experience but also the realities of the dominant group as well. This is not a choice. Success in a society that both centers and conveys value upon dominant cultural values requires everyone's participation. People of color have to navigate the very real consequences of racist systems, often starting at a very young age. As a result, people of color are uniquely positioned to see both the privileges that the dominant group enjoys as well as the lack thereof. James Baldwin said, "You cannot lynch me and keep me in ghettos without becoming something monstrous yourselves. And furthermore, you give me a terrifying advantage. You never had to look at me. I had to look at you. I know more about you than you know about me."[12] He is describing his position in the standpoint theory.

Over time, people of color have developed and utilized our cultural wealth to navigate the obstacles placed in our path and to make up for the disparities created by privilege. While this is certainly an asset, and one that educators should capitalize upon, these skills and abilities are not a substitution for erasing unearned disadvantages. An issue that is central to the maintenance of racist systems is the fact that the people who see the least also typically have the closest proximity to power. Even leaders with the best intentions might fall victim to the gaps in their vision, which is why it is so important that we involve key stakeholders in our students' lives when making important decisions about their education.

We see this in schools when students, parents, and community members are shut out of decision-making. Parents and families are our partners in the education of their children. It is not enough to get parents and guardians involved as a reactive response when students aren't meeting expectations. Families should be a core part of the fabric of the school, which means that we are most successful when we engage with them proactively and give them a seat at the table. We do ourselves no favors when we isolate the people who should be our greatest allies in the mission of educating their children.

Envisioning Equity

Before equity can be a reality in our schools and classrooms, we first have to envision what it looks like. In schools it is easy to be socialized into a scarcity mindset. Educators are asked to accomplish massive tasks with minor budgets, to teach years' worth of content in a matter of months, and to do all of that while catering to the social and emotional needs of our students. Existing in this reality for a long period of time can condition us to think far more about what we don't have, or what's not possible, than it conditions us to dream of the possibilities.

Overcoming Racism workshops incorporate an activity where we ask our participants to envision what equity would look like for different groups of students. Participants complete this brainstorming in the absence of budget constraints, in a scenario where their school has unlimited resources. One would think that this condition would make the activity easier, but what we see play out almost every time in these workshops is that dreaming outside of a budget is the most difficult part of the exercise for educators. We don't remove the budget constraints because we want our participants to live in a utopian fantasy world. We move those constraints because learning to envision and actualize change requires a level of imagination that is frequently beaten out of us in our first few years in the classroom. Once we stop being able to imagine the possibilities, we lose one of our most important tools in the fight to overcome opportunity gaps.

Cultivating classrooms that see and value student's cultural wealth starts with envisioning a school that does this effectively. We can always pair down our approach to be in alignment with our resources and limitations. It is far more difficult to see the possibilities when we start with a scarcity mindset.

Notes

1. Howard Zinn, *You Can't Be Neutral on a Moving Train: A Personal History of Our Times* (Boston: Beacon Press, 1994).

2. Tara J. Yosso, "Whose Culture Has Capital? A Critical Race Theory Discussion of Community Cultural Wealth," *Race Ethnicity and Education* 8, no. 1 (2005): 77.

3. Ibid., 77.

4. Ibid., 78, 79.

5. Ibid., 79.

6. Ibid., 79, 80.

7. Ibid., 80.

8. Ibid., 80.

9. Brenda J. Allen, "Feminist Standpoint Theory: A Black Woman's (Re) View of Organizational Socialization," *Communication Studies* 47, no. 4 (1996): 257–71, https://doi.org/10.1080/10510979609368482.

10. "Diversity in Medicine: Facts and Figures 2019," Association of American Medical Colleges, n.d., https://www.aamc.org/data-reports/work force/report/diversity-medicine-facts-and-figures-2019.

11. Beverly Daniel Tatum, "The Complexity of Identity: Who Am I?," in *Readings for Diversity and Social Justice: An Anthology on Racism, Sexism, Anti-Semitism, Heterosexism, Classism and Ableism*, ed. Maurianne Adams, Warren J. Blumenfeld, Carmelita (Rosie) Castañeda, Heather W. Hackman, Madeline L. Peters, and Ximena Zúñiga (New York: Routledge, 2018), 9–14; see also https://uucsj.org/wp-content/uploads/2016/05/The-Complexity-of-Identity.pdf. Tatum cites Jean B. Miller, "Domination and Subordination," in *Toward a New Psychology of Women* (Boston: Beacon Press, 1976), 8.

12. James Baldwin, quoted in Raoul Peck's documentary *I Am Not Your Negro* (Magnolia Pictures, 2016). Also quoted in "I Am Not Your Negro: James Baldwin's View on the Reality of America," by Amata, *Journey of a 21st-Century Afrikan Queen* (blog), October 27, 2017, https://giramatans.wordpress.com/2017/10/27/i-am-not-your-negro-james-baldwins-view-on-the-reality-of-america/.

Chapter 9

Oh Freedom: Staying on the Battlefield

We started this book by talking about intention. What is your why? What is going to keep us committed to the radical reimagination of our education system, especially when this work feels challenging and unfamiliar. Regardless of where you are in your journey, this work will feel challenging because change is hard. It will likely feel unfamiliar because we are trying to do things differently in a system that is often stubborn and resistant to change. Countless scholars and educators have paved the way, and still the journey for equity is a long and often arduous process. We have to ask ourselves: Is this a battle worth fighting? And if it is, what are we willing to sacrifice in order to see it through? Until we cover the distance between our fears and our faith, the goals we aim to accomplish are meaningless. Assata Shakur reminds us that "dreams and reality are opposites. Action synthesizes them."[1] Ultimately our actions define our values and our actions will define the outcomes for the students we serve.

When I was 14 years old, an educator by the name of Charisse Jackson took me under her wing and taught me how to harness my passion for change. I met Charisse at a youth leadership program called Anytown. I grew up in St. Louis, Missouri, and Anytown in St. Louis gathered kids from all over the city and every walk of life. There were wealthy kids, working-class kids, kids from what felt like every racial categorization, trans kids, cis kids, straight kids, gay kids. To this day, Anytown is the most diverse environment that I ever had the pleasure to exist in. The thing I admired most about Anytown was that it created an environment that was a model for the world to mimic, rather than creating an environment that mimicked the world. In schools we sometimes become so focused on preparing students for the "real world" that we forget that we are the ones raising the next generation, the generation of leaders who will define what the "real world" is. At Anytown we learned about the interconnectedness of oppression. With each passing day we received opportunities to learn from each other's experiences and opportunities to atone for our own complicity in unjust systems. I cannot think of any way to describe Anytown other than liberating. Every summer in high school for eight days I was given the opportunity to live in the world that I wanted to see become a reality.

On the last day of Anytown there was a familiar tradition. Charisse addressed the assembled student delegates wearing army fatigue pants and gave a life-changing speech. Before she spoke she played a song, a "negro spiritual" called "Stay on the Battlefield," performed by Sweet Honey in the Rock. The first time I heard it I immediately recognized it because my grandmother used to sing it. My father had nine siblings, which meant that I had more cousins than I am interested in counting. Every summer we would descend upon my grandparents' farm, and even though my grandparents didn't have a lot of money, one thing was certain: we were going to eat well while we were there. My grandmother or grandfather would cook us breakfast every morning—sausage, rice, eggs, and occasionally bacon. When my grandmother cooked for us in the morning, I remember her singing that song. "I am going to stay on the battlefield." Hearing it again for the first time in years brought tears to my eyes.

Once the song ended, Charisse began to speak. She talked about the choice that sat in front of us, the choice to join the generations-long battle for justice or the choice to stay on the sideline as a bystander. At 14 years old I thought the choice was clear. Of course I wanted to commit my life to fighting for a better world for people who looked like me and for people who lived in targeted identities that I did not share. As the years have passed and as I have grown older, I now realize that this commitment is much more difficult than I could have ever imagined. Choosing to do what is right simply because it is the right thing to do has caused me more pain and anguish than perhaps any other decision I have made in my life. If systems and structures wanted to change, then changing them would be easier. So as Charisse played the song that I remembered from my grandmother, I began to listen to the lyrics:

> *I'm gonna stay on the battlefield*
> *I'm gonna stay on the battlefield*
> *I'm gonna stay on the battlefield til I die.*

Then the second chorus went:

> *I'm gonna treat everybody right*
> *I'm gonna treat everybody right*
> *I'm gonna treat everybody right til I die.*

The last chorus repeated the first:

> *I'm gonna stay on the battlefield*
> *I'm gonna stay on the battlefield*
> *I'm gonna stay on the battlefield til I die.*

This song started out as a Christian hymn but was adapted to be a freedom song, as many "negro spirituals" were. When my grandmother sang this song it was about faith—faith that, despite the harsh reality that Black people had to live in throughout her life, things would be better for the generations that followed as long as she stayed on the battlefield. As a kid it was very difficult for me to understand the meaning of the lyrics. I wondered why the people who were the victims of persecution were also the ones who sang about treating others right and ushering in justice. It wasn't until Charisse's speech reminded me of the song that I began to understand.

The work that we have ahead of us is not about us. The work isn't even solely about our students. The work that we are embarking on is about the consciousness of humanity as a whole. It is about loving one another enough to understand that our freedom and unfreedom are intertwined. The reason my grandmother could sing about treating others right in the midst of her own persecution was because she understood that injustice is the byproduct of brokenness, fear, confusion, and ultimately pain. As James Baldwin so incisively put it, "One of the reasons people cling to their hates so stubbornly is because they sense, once hate is gone, they will be forced to deal with pain."[2] Freedom songs were the soundtrack of the Civil Rights Movement. They offered instruction, motivation, and hope in the midst of a battle that seemed impossible. When I find myself mired in pessimism because of today's political climate, I remind myself of what people who fought for freedom endured in the generations before me. We don't really sing freedom songs anymore, which is a shame because the journey ahead of us will require all of the guidance, strength, and hope that we can muster.

Freedom Song

In my classroom we studied the Civil Rights Movement and freedom movements across the world. The sit-in movement in the United States is always one of my favorite things to expose my students to, in part because it was led by young people. It stands as one of the most effective civil disobedience campaigns in the history of the United States, and it was meticulously planned, organized, and executed. Studying the sit-in movement was like giving my students a master class on transformative resistance. One of the elements that was most striking to my students was how well dressed the protesters were. They analyzed the images of the protesters being beaten and spat upon. They saw white mobs pour condiments on their clothes, they saw them bleeding from the bludgeoning that they received.

As 12- and 13-year-olds in New Orleans, the students struggled to process why the protesters chose not to fight back, and even more so why they wore their best clothes to be assaulted in. I explained to them that civil disobedience was about drawing attention to their cause. They felt that in order to get white audiences across the country to care about the injustices Black Americans faced, they had to put their "best foot forward." In order for the protesters to get the attention and sympathy necessary to change the laws, white Americans needed to see them beaten in a suit while studying and doing their homework at a public lunch counter. The theory of change was that, when the media saw these young activists being brutalized, the images would humanize them.

For years in schools our reform efforts have aimed to do the same thing. We are very good at putting our kids in a "suit." We teach our students how to talk a certain way, how to dress a certain way, how to sit a certain way, how to exist in public spaces a certain way. The belief is that if our students master the skills of assimilation, then perhaps society will show them the empathy that they deserve. So much of our work to reform schools has landed as efforts to reform kids, when in reality our kids were never the problem to begin with. As we exist in a time in which white supremacy is becoming as vocal as it has ever been, some of us are coming to the understanding that white supremacy is more stubborn than many of us believed. I have watched brilliant students perform perfectly within the norms and expectations of the dominant society and still not have access to the choices that they worked for and should have earned. As the systems that we are facing have evolved, it is time for us to evolve as well. Perhaps it is not enough to prepare our students to have dignity and poise in the midst of injustice. Perhaps there are lessons that we can learn from other elements of the Civil Rights Movement that are not as widely discussed.

This brings me back to the freedom songs, like the one my grandmother used to sing and that Charisse played to close out our time at Anytown. While the suits and the formal wear were about the outward image being projected to the world, freedom songs were for the activists, freedom songs were about building cultural competence, freedom songs were about building self-esteem, freedom songs were about building pride in identity and who we are. At times when faith was all that civil rights activists had to lean on, they turned to songs that were once rooted in their faith. The key points were embedded in the lyrics and the rhythm and these songs provide the roadmap for the movement. I recommend that you take some time to listen to the lyrics of some of these songs.

"Ain't Gonna Let Nobody Turn Me Around"

> *Ain't gonna let nobody turn me around,*
> *Turn me around, turn me around.*
> *Ain't gonna let nobody turn me around,*
> *I'm gonna keep on walkin', keep on talkin'*
> *Marchin' down to freedom land.*

"We Shall Overcome"

> *We shall overcome, we shall overcome,*
> *We shall overcome some day.*
> *Oh deep in my heart, I do believe,*
> *We shall overcome some day.*

"Oh Freedom"

> *Oh freedom! Oh, freedom!*
> *Oh, freedom over me!*
> *Before I be a slave*
> *I'll be buried in my grave*
> *And go home to my Lord and be free.*

"We Shall Not be Moved"

> *We shall not, we shall not be moved.*
> *Like a tree that's planted by the water,*

We shall not be moved.
We are fighting for our children,
We shall not be moved.
Just like a tree that's planted by the water,
We shall not be moved.

"Keep Your Eyes on the Prize"

Hold on, hold on, hold, hold on,
Keep your eyes on the prize, hold on.

We sang freedom songs after harrowing defeats to renew our spirits. We sang freedom songs after resounding victories to buoy the charge ahead. We sang freedom songs in jail cells and while marching in the streets. In the midst of situations that seemed insurmountable, these songs provided just a little bit of fuel to the people who remained steadfast in their commitment to justice.

When I think about what it means to provide a song to students, I find that we often do a good job with motion. We don't always do a great job of action. Dr. Lerone Bennett Jr. once said:

> There can be no revolutionary movement . . . without revolutionary conception grounded in our realities. It is very important for us not to confuse motion with action. Motion is the movement of limbs and lips without a plan. Action is motion informed by thought. The most urgent problem of the hour is ideological clarity. In fact, strategic thinking of a depth and intensity unparalleled in our history has become a matter of life and death.[3]

He ends the quote by asking, "What are we doing?" We frequently get so caught up in our desire to do good that we don't sit down to plan out what doing good looks like. What is the end goal that we want to accomplish and what will it take to get there? How can we not focus solely on preparing our students to navigate the injustice of the world but focus on preparing a world that is worthy of our students? While we may not have power to change all of the systems that operate in society, we have the power and agency to change the systems that govern our schools and classrooms.

We have an obligation to envelop our students with love and to give them the skills, tools, and knowledge necessary to fully actualize their freedom. How are the lessons that we plan intentional? How do we give our students meaningful and rigorous tasks? The reality is that no matter how we teach our students to speak and dress, they are still going to go out and face a world that might prejudge them. The power in the freedom song is that the opponents of justice can't beat it, or spit on it, or pour ketchup on it, because the songs live within us and within our students.

If there is one thing that I know very well, it is that it can feel like the work that we do is in vain. That no matter how hard we work and no matter how hard we fight, nothing will ever truly change. The intentionality of what we put in front of kids matters, and in the midst of all of the noise surrounding our work it can be easy to forget to listen to the music. The music of our students' pencils gliding over their papers. The music of their laughter and joy. The music of their hands banging on desks and lunch tables. The music in their hope, their curiosity, their aspirations, and their faith. If we allow the noise to drown out the music, then the freedom that we seek our students to live in will drift further and further away. We have to prepare our students for this world, and if this world might choose to be unkind to our kids, it is our responsibility— whether it is fair to us or not—to give our students the armor that they need to sustain and to navigate those environments.

Education is one of the greatest tools of resistance that our kids will have. As Nelson Mandela once said, "Education is the most powerful weapon which you can use to change the word."[4] This means that we have to be intentional about teaching our students the truth and letting them grapple with that and to provide them with that song that will hopefully carry their spirit even when it feels like there is darkness all around.

School systems that serve children of color often prioritize assimilation as a vehicle for achievement. Appeals to white morality and consciousness constitute a primary vehicle for success. This shows up in "character education" programming, strict dress codes, and policies that restrict voice and movement, as well as exclusionary discipline policies. The myth of meritocracy also lives in these policies that advocate assimilation as the only vehicle for upward mobility. We must provide students with the tools to envision and actualize a better world for themselves and their peers around them. The characteristics present in freedom songs provide us with a great baseline to do just that:

- Call and response: This culturally affirming method of communication promotes mutual participation and collective responsibility.
- Aspirational capital: The world doesn't have to be static; we have the power to make change.
- Resistant capital: Education is a tool of resistance that can be transformative rather than self-defeating.
- Culturally sustaining: Our education can sustain our culture. Dr. Jeff Duncan Andrade compares culture to medicine. How can we create and maintain an education system that keeps us from getting sick from the virus that is systemic oppression?

On Hope

Paulo Freire said, "It is imperative to maintain hope even when the harshness of reality suggests the opposite."[5] Along your journey of implementing the things that you learned in this book, there will be many moments and events that might make you feel hopeless. Even when it feels like things are not going our way, hope is the light that marks our path. There is a reason why I founded Overcoming Racism to be an organization that primarily works with educators. I am not sure that the bankers will wake up tomorrow and decide collectively to work on income or wealth inequality. I don't believe the oil companies will come together in the next few weeks or months to take on climate change. I don't think our politicians are going to work together across political differences to pass policies that over time eliminate the systemic dynamics of oppression. I started doing this work in education because as educators we have a very powerful catalyst for change that we all happen to share. That catalyst is our students. Regardless of an educator's background, political leanings, religious beliefs, or anything other identity that defines them, educators come into this underfunded and overworked profession because they want to see their students succeed. There is something special about the sacrifices that educators make on behalf of their students. Somewhere deep inside of ourselves where our collective love for our students resides is the key to overcoming racism in education.

In the end, I believe that we will win this battle for equity in education because winning is literally the only choice that we have. If we love our students, truly love them the way that we say that we do, then standing by while the status quo plays out and students are left behind is not even an option. When we take away the possibility of failing to accomplish our goal, then we have no choice but to work toward it together. We have no choice but to stay on the battlefield until all of our students are fully free.

Notes

1. Assata Shakur, *Assata: An Autobiography* (Chicago: Lawrence Hill Books, 2001).

2. James Baldwin, *Notes of a Native Son* (London: Penguin Classics, 2017), 597.

3. Lerone Bennett Jr., *The Challenge of Blackness* (Chicago: Johnson Publishing Company, 1972), 23.

4. Nelson Mandela, "Address by Nelson Mandela at launch of Mindset Network, Johannesburg," July 16, 2003, Nelson Mandela Foundation, http://www.mandela.gov.za/mandela_speeches/2003/030716_mindset.htm.

5. Paulo Freire, quoted in bell hooks, *Teaching Community: A Pedagogy of Hope* (New York: Routledge, 2003), 13.

About the Author

Matthew Kincaid has been teaching and leading anti-racism work since he was 14 years old. Matthew is an educator driven by his commitment to revolutionize education so that it works for every child. With a background as a teacher, school administrator, instructional coach, and consultant, his life's work has been to forge a transformative education system. As the visionary force behind Overcoming Racism, Matthew empowers schools and businesses with race and equity professional development, guidance, and support. In his capacity as the founder and CEO of Overcoming Racism, he has trained thousands of educators and business and community leaders. His work focuses on identifying and changing systems that perpetuate injustice within organizations. He has been showcased in a number of prestigious platforms, including the *Washington Post, Forbes,* the *Huffington Post, Now This,* and *Black Enterprise,* amplifying the message of equitable education for all.

Acknowledgments

I am thankful that I was raised in a praying family, and that I was taught that all things are possible through faith. I believe that anti-racism work is a ministry and I wouldn't be here without God.

I would like to thank everyone who has dedicated their life to making the world a more just and equitable place. Thank you for your freedom songs. Thank you for paving a path for me to follow. Thank you for daring to believe that change is possible and worth fighting for.

I would like to thank my mom, Susan Kincaid, and my dad, Basil Kincaid. There are no words to describe how grateful I am for you two. You raised my brother and me with love and compassion and you instilled in us both the will to follow our dreams. You are more than parents—you are my friends, my confidantes, and my trusted advisors. You have made countless sacrifices, sometimes going without to ensure that I had the things that I needed. Thank you for always believing in me and pointing me in the direction of my dreams and supporting me along the way. I hope you look at how far we have come and recognize that none of this happens without the two of you. I love you.

To Basil ("Naw, that's Lil Basil"): Your creativity, artistry, and work ethic are unmatched. You inspire me in so many ways. From playing videogames on the living room floor to attending your international art shows, whenever we are together it is a good time. You have supported me over the years in more ways than I can count. Thank you for being both my big brother and my best friend. Thank you for being such a bright light that when I am around you, I cannot help but shine. I love you bro. Thank you.

Share: Without you this book doesn't get done. You have been patient, kind, and supportive. In the beginning of this process, I wasn't clear on the type of support I needed. You listened, you adapted, but most importantly you always showed up. Thank you for constantly reminding me of who I am and how great I can be when I have the right people alongside of me. Thank you for making space for me during the times when this process was hard on me and for providing me with the love and acceptance that I needed to see this though. I love and appreciate you.

Charisse: At 14 years old you gave me a purpose and a platform to learn and teach about anti-racism. You changed my life and so many others and for that I thank you.

Ahmed and Courtney: Thank you for holding down the fort and continuing to guide Overcoming Racism as I worked on the book. Thank you for reading and reviewing chapters and lending your brilliant brains to me to brainstorm book names, chapter names, and cover art. Thank you for showing up for me every time I needed you.

To my aunts and uncles: I love each and every one of you all and I truly feel the love that you have for me. Each one of you have impacted my life in a different way and the sum of all of your support is a big part of who I am. Thank you for being who you are and for making this family so special and such a powerful force in my life.

My cousins: You know who you are. Thank you for the laughs, the support, and the reminder to keep the heart of a lion under pressure.

Daniel, Khalid and Cyrus: Thank you for always being a listening ear and a constant support in all of the things I have done. Our brotherhood gives me the confidence to boldly pursue my dreams. I appreciate you always standing by me as I continue in this journey.

Joe Brown, John Pope and the Rho Nu Chapter: Thank you for being such a positive influence on me during such a developmental stage in my life. Thank you for introducing me to a brotherhood that not only lifelong but eternal. Thank you for inspiring me, pushing me, believing in me and supporting me along the way.

India: You taught me what it meant to love students unconditionally and to make the spaces for them that they deserve. Thank you.

Troy: You taught me to take my work seriously but not to take myself too seriously while doing the work. Thank you.

Traciamanda: For being the first person to believe in Overcoming Racism and for opening doors for this organization to exist, thank you.

Meinig: You gave me my first job in the classroom and you allowed me to do it my way. Whenever you have had the opportunity to do so, you continued opening doors for me and supported my work. Thank you!

Ced, Erika, Brooklyn, Braxton, and Brock: Thank you for your continued love and support. Blood could not make us closer and your love, support and guidance has been essential to the man I have become.

Dean Hollister and Mindy Nierenberg: For always believing in me and supporting me to overcome one of the most difficult obstacles I've faced in my life, thank you.

Amy Fandrei and Wiley Publishing: Thank you for believing in me. Thank you for investing in me. Thank you for making accommodations that made this process work for me.

Amy Handy: Thank you for reading my book with so much intentionality. You have a wise and kind spirit and I am so grateful that you were my copy editor.

Sal LaRocca: Thank you for your kind words and well wishes throughout this process and your faith in me that my work can change the world around me.

Overcoming Racism Partners: Without you all, nothing exists. To everyone who has ever attended an Overcoming Racism workshop or brought us in to do a training or workshop at your school or organization, thank you!

Index